COSMIC DEPUTY

COSMIC DEPUTY

poetry and context 1968-2019

KALAMU YA SALAAM

THE UNIVERSITY OF NEW ORLEANS PRESS
RUNAGATE PRESS

Cosmic Deputy:
poetry and context 1968-2019

Runagate Press
University of New Orleans Press
Manufactured in the United States of America

Cover photo by Alex Lear (Alexandra Jones), shot in the studio of Brandan "B-Mike" Odums
Book and cover design by Alex Dimeff

Library of Congress Cataloging-in-Publication Data

Names: Salaam, Kalamu ya, 1947- author.
Title: Cosmic deputy : poetry and context 1968-2019 / Kalamu ya Salaam.
Description: First edition. | New Orleans : The University of New Orleans Press ; Runagate Press, 2020. | Includes index.
Identifiers: LCCN 2020035278 (print) | LCCN 2020035279 (ebook) | ISBN 9781608011896 (paperback ; acid-free paper) | ISBN 9781608011940 (ebook)

Subjects: LCGFT: Essays. | Poetry.
Classification: LCC PS3561.A4162 C67 2020 (print) | LCC PS3561.A4162 (ebook) | DDC 811/.54--dc23
LC record available at https://lccn.loc.gov/2020035278
LC ebook record available at https://lccn.loc.gov/2020035279

First edition 2020
Printed on acid-free paper

RUNAGATE PRESS

THE UNIVERSITY OF NEW ORLEANS PRESS
2000 Lakeshore Drive
Earl K. Long Library, Room 221
New Orleans, LA 70148
United States
504-280-7457
unopress.org

First to my father and mother
Big Val (Vallery Ferdinand Jr.)
'Nola (Inola Copelin Ferdinand)
they made me
physically, psychologically and spiritually

Second to my junior high school teachers
particularly my English teacher
Mrs. O. E. Nelson
my industrial arts teacher
Mr. Conrad

Thirdly to my triumvirate of patron saints
Langston Hughes (first and always)
James Baldwin
Amiri Baraka

CONTENTS

INDEX

PREFACE: PERFECTION OF BEAUTY

by Afaa M. Weaver

Afaa Michael Weaver was a factory worker in Baltimore for fifteen years before publishing his first collection of poetry, Water Song, *in 1985. He has since published several books and received numerous fellowships and awards, including a Fulbright Scholar appointment to Taiwan in 2002. Weaver is currently a member of the core faculty in the Drew MFA program in Poetry and Poetry in Translation.*

In the tenderest of moments, the poetry of Kalamu ya Salaam, opens to reveal an inner steadfastness, a spirit planted deeply inside a faith in the beauty of blackness, a sensibility that informs an erudite critical reasoning that eschews anything that would diminish the sacredness of Black culture. In *Cosmic Deputy*, we have the cartography of a celestial system that lives in the mind of a poet who has seen the world and had the world inscribed inside him in miniature while growing up in New Orleans in the community known as the Mighty Nine. New Orleans is host to Congo Square, where African Americans gathered to celebrate and weave together the fabric of their several cultures as they were ripped from their contexts and sent sailing over the Atlantic to be enslaved. They wove and they prayed. They chanted and they invoked the cosmos in their various perceptions. They reasoned, they felt, they endured. It is in this faith in residence that Kalamu ya Salaam has taken on the fractal realties of the world in which we live, one that holds fast in often inscrutable ways to its adversarial relationship with Black life. *Cosmic Deputy* is the work of the poet as cultural steward. These poems sing with the vulnerability of confession, the variations of jazz and the blues, the African concept of cool, and the miracle of African people and their descendants honoring these legacies, a continuity that is itself pure genius.

Much of the tone of his work is in the priestly mode of attending to spiritual presence and ritualistic use of the powers of invocation and appeasement in a secular making of literary art. His compass is rooted in the not so simple concept of respect. "My Story, My Song" is one of several way stations where the travelers are those of the powerfully disembodied, the ancestral host, and the poet walks with them in his meditations:

> if you don't mind not knowing what dust god molded you
> from
> then you can go head on and not know the blues, but me
> myself,
> i carries my past deep inside my dream pocket

In the unveiling of his aesthetic, the poet struts his virtuoso weaving and romping through English, code-switching as some might say, or shifting the harmonics if we keep to music, which is a central thread of Kalamu's sensibility, his witnessing.

His mother was a teacher, which may partly account for his belief in instruction, not too unlike similar ideas in theater, and in that way Kalamu's work is in alignment with the emergence of the blues sensibility in early hip hop. He speaks directly to Black people in his distinctive cadence, encapsulating drum and song, transmitting information over thousands of miles and galaxies of heartache in those who did not survive the Middle Passage, and those who did. I imagine his mother's affirmation of his desire to be a writer from a very early age is key to his commitment to stewardship. He writes for one primary reward, to do what his ancestral awareness has said is his mission, to show that blackness is not pathological but a heroic corrective to the national pathology of American culture that threatens all of us.

In "4 Haiku, My Philosophy," he puts forth a philosophy that the body of his work shows is not diminished by accommodations made to skeptics, inner or outer. "haiku #58" has a sterling clarity in a language nuanced by the subtleties of Black religiosity, formal and secular:

black people believe
in god, & i believe in
black people, amen

The Zen terseness as it appears at times in his work is evidence of an awakening he explains elsewhere as what happened during his military service in the time of the War in Vietnam. Salaam was stationed on a mountaintop in South Korea, about fifty miles from the DMZ before returning to New Orleans and the Black Power Movement. He gives the reader his credo in explicit terms, mapping the terrain of an unapologetic self-love. We see the secular strategy of poet as warrior-priest.

Cosmic Deputy is reminiscent of Melvin B. Tolson's *A Gallery of Harlem Portraits*, but where Tolson displays a critical tone mixed with his affection for his subject, Kalamu's love for his subject is unabashed. He eschews the trickster's mysterious air for deliberate expressions, and is, in that way, more reminiscent of Ogun, the fiery weapons maker of the Yoruba cosmology than of Eshu, whose trickster tactics resemble the principle of uncertainty more than the idea of witch doctors popularized by Europeans. Kalamu's poetry also bears the mark of the influence of Margaret Walker, whose "For My People" is the poetic companion to "Lift Every Voice and Sing." The cadence in Walker's long lines, her musicality in marshaling Black culture are things that Kalamu inherits. A third influence is, I think, the most significant because the tradition chose him when he was just a boy. Langston Hughes became the poet's patron saint when he was in the 8th grade, and the patronage is everywhere evident in Kalamu's devotion to African American culture.

Inspired by Hughes' life work, his spirit mission of breathing the culture of his people into literary art aims to be a body of the dignity of cultural self. Conferring deputy status on those who apply, Kalamu outlines the cosmic duties as he writes:

all cosmic deputies must commit
a minimum of fifty-five
random acts of kindness a day, must be
unceasing in freely offering
unprovoked displays of beauty

The conferring of duties is as grand as Sun Ra's explications of the joy of interplanetary travel, or the inner revelations of Bob Kaufman's silences. Beauty is a trope that rides the waves of the electromagnetic fields emitted from Kalamu's summoning from inside the regional capital of Black culture that is New Orleans, where his commitment and his art have earned him the title of revered father, friend and mentor, one who sends poems singing from the interior, his and our own.

It is life, as such, which the poet comes to see as his essential mission. The inner sanctum is the poet's complex heart, and in the grand orchestral movement that is Kalamu ya Salaam's poetic, we see his love of African American culture is his love of New Orleans, and his love of New Orleans is his embodiment of the precious history of Black people.

He posits his literary art in a geography that emanates from a southern center in this country and southward more to the Caribbean and Latin America, where the vast majority of Africans were taken in Maafa, the African holocaust that became the sacrifice offered to the insatiable mouth of greed. His work stands staunch in the face of a history that has dared Black voices to see their own, with a steadfastness that gathered strength in his contact with Asia, where he was shown the larger extension of the struggle he inherited at birth, an inheritance as opposed to a birthright. Centered in the present, fixed inside the inner sanctum of the poet's being, the divine breath lives in the infinite space of hard-won understanding, where it takes courage to accept the unknowable outcomes of our lives.

In a time that now lives in myth, a Black man stood on the porch of his home and watched as a car eased down the dirt path to his house, managing the twists and turns around the edges of the line of grass that seemed to pull the car along as if it were hitched to the air going over the soft tops of the leaves. The dust accumulated and then rolled out to the side and thinned out into nothing. The car pulled into the yard. Another Black man stepped out and stood there looking at the man on the porch, who was indeed himself, as the man on the porch recognized the driver as himself.

If we meet ourselves in the later years and know ourselves, we are blessed with poetry's grace. What a poet can expect in his later years is not something that can be easily prophesied, if it can be prophesied at all. There is the infinite turning of chance, where the very least a poet can hope for is to arrive in these later years with a wealth of clarity and good health. Beyond that all is gift, and the wealth of work, the size and breadth of it that Kalamu ya Salaam offers in this collection of his poetry is the gift not just to him, but to the reader. We are, dear reader, so fortunate because the poet has seen himself, in his own struggle to be, and known himself. It is this grace that no poet can force, and every culture is the better for having poets who make the journey and come home to themselves and to us.

Afaa M. Weaver 尉雅風

COSMIC DEPUTY

ESSAYS

WHAT IS POETRY?

I have sometimes joked with some of my novel-writing friends that I can define what poetry is; can you define what the novel is? Other than the general statement that a novel is a long story, there is no definitive definition of the novel as a major literary form. In contradistinction, poetry, which is often considered the oldest genre of literature, is easily defined as a form that employs one or more of four specific elements:

1. Line length as determined by the poet rather than by the medium within which it exists.

Depending on the size of the page, the width of a particular prose selection will change, but with poetry, the line length remains the same regardless of the size of the medium.

2. The specific use of sound as an essential element.

Sound elements are those you hear when the poem is articulated aloud. Even when read silently to one's self, the sound of the poem is still heard inside one's head. The four most frequently employed sound elements are rhyme, assonance/consonance, alliteration and onomatopoeia.

3. The conscious employment of meter and/or rhythm.

4. Figurative language, chiefly similes and metaphors.

I believe all poetry started off as speech rather than text, and in the case of Black culture, poetry is strongly informed by music and public performance.

A HALF CENTURY OF POETRY

How does one sum up over fifty years of poetry that was written under widely divergent circumstances?

I composed the poems in this collection between the years of 1968, when I came out of the Army and began working with the Free Southern Theatre, and 2020, co-terminus with the death of my second wife, Beaula "Nia" McCoy, on February 28 of that year.

I seldom date my writings. Years afterwards it is virtually impossible to put the work in chronological order. Additionally, my work did not develop in a linear way from fledgling to professional. All my styles and genres appeared in my earliest poems, circa 1968—except for haiku poems, which I began writing circa 1985. Although there are not many haiku included here, I have literally written hundreds of haiku.

In putting together *Cosmic Deputy*, I decided to combine two organizational approaches. First, this collection presents poems that have appeared in my own books in order of publication. Second, it presents an alphabetically arranged grouping of poems, the bulk of which, although often performed, were not included in my previous books. I should note that a number of these poems were published on my numerous internet blogs, as well as in diverse journals, newspapers and anthologies.

This approach to organizing my poetic work has both strengths and weaknesses, especially for scholars who attempt to analyze or categorize my work. But it is what it is. This is the book that represents my half century-plus of poetic work.

My poetry is further introduced in the next section, "Art For Life: My Story, My Song," a long and detailed essay/thesis that offers my approach to poetry. *Cosmic Deputy* is both my theory and my practice of poetry.

ART FOR LIFE: MY STORY, MY SONG

this is my story
my song, i will sing these blues,
tho they stole my tongue

I was born Vallery Ferdinand III on 24 March 1947 in New Orleans, Louisiana. My early publishing is done under the name of Val Ferdinand. In 1970, I changed my name to Kalamu ya Salaam (Pen of Peace).

Because I do a great deal of writing as a journalist, music producer (scripting radio programs, album liner notes and artist bios), dramatist, cultural critic, propagandist for various issues, fiction writer and advertising executive, I usually shy away from identifying myself with any one genre of writing. Poetry is, however, my most developed and my most comfortable voice.

I consider poetry the song of literature and consider myself a griot, an African American praise-singer who resounds with the voice and vision of my people.

one: in the beginning

> *I think the best thing I can do at this time is to try to get myself in shape and know myself. If I can do that, then I'll just play, you see, and leave it at that. I believe that will do it, if I really can get to myself and be just as I feel I should be and play it.*
>
> *—John William Coltrane*

Today I am a poet, but I did not choose poetry; poetry found me. I was in eighth grade; Mrs. O. E. Nelson baptized me. I had been in the water before, but until that day I had never gotten religion.

I was familiar with poetry through church, as well as through segregated public schools where Black teachers, mostly female, imparted culture in both subtle and overt ways. I will never forget the opening lines of William Ernest Henley's poem "Invictus": "out of the night that covers me / black as the pit from pole to pole / I thank whatever gods may be / for my unconquerable soul."

"Invictus" is not a "Black" poem, but the poem has special meaning when done "Blackly," as it was under the tutelage of Mrs. Wilson, my sixth-grade teacher at Phillis Wheatley elementary school.

Although our rowdy class had once sent a student teacher fleeing out of the classroom in tears, Mrs. Wilson had the power to render us dumb, to leave us literally holding our breaths and not daring to say a mumbling word when she confronted us. One day after lunch, as we settled into our seats, she wrote "pussy" in big, bold letters across the blackboard. She asked us, any of us, to define "pussy."

I don't know why she chose that word, but it was a powerful lesson that culminated with one of the young ladies in the class reading out loud the dictionary definitions about pussy willows and pet names for cats, etc.

We all knew that the meaning of the word according to Webster was not the issue. Mrs. Wilson cared enough about us to force us to deal with defining ourselves. Even though after school we laughed and exchanged, in whispered conspiracy, other definitions, still from that moment, we became, probably for the first time in most of our young lives, conscious of the need to define what we meant when we used a word. We had been challenged to take responsibility for every word we said.

Far more than solely academics, Mrs. Wilson taught pride to a classroom of Black youngsters who ranged in hue from the light-skinned "Creoles" (as mulattos are generally referred to among Blacks in New Orleans) to dark-skinned folk.

I had classmates who would pass for White on the city's public buses after school. We'd get on together; however, the darker-skinned of us would sit in the back behind the "colored" signs. We sometimes threw those "colored screens" out the window, but those were the rare sometimes. In general, we just trooped on to the back of the bus and followed the convention of the day, the convention that also meant our fairer-skinned schoolmates sat up front, passing for White. Somehow, we knew there was no hard feelings. Some people could run faster than others. Some people were smarter at spelling or English or whatever, and some people were light enough to pass for White.

At the time, we did not see "passing" as a particular pathology because this was still public school, and everybody was from the same or similar economic strata. Later that would change, but for now we were all laughing, awkward adolescents who were made to stand in the front of the classroom and recite, with feeling, the concluding lines of "Invictus": "I am the master of my fate / I am the captain of my soul."

By eighth grade, while I had already been ushered into poetry as a social upliftment device, I did not yet have a conscious knowledge of "nommo" even though I had felt "the force of the orated word" as manifested by preachers in the church, and by the brothers talking shit on the block, and also by the recitations that were an integral part of our education at that time.

We were taught Black poetry, such as "If We Must Die" by Claude McKay, "God's Trombones" by James Weldon Johnson and "When Malindy Sings" by Paul Lawrence Dunbar. Yet I did not define all those oratorical touchstones, which I knew by heart, as poetry. They weren't poetry like the poetry we studied from books, the Shakespeare and stuff. Our textbooks concentrated on White worlds, and I associated poetry with that world.

The stuff I learned by heart and loved didn't come to me via a book. Most often those works came by word of mouth and by listening. Occasionally, a poem was runoff on a sheet of paper and passed around for us to learn and recite.

Moreover, I never thought of reciting Shakespeare in the same way that we recited James Weldon Johnson. This was probably the beginnings of my belief that Black poetry must be heard to be fully appreciated. I know there are people who feel that way about Shakespeare, but Shakespeare's rhythms did not quicken my blood.

At the gut level—the blood pounding, getting excited, aroused, your heart literally racing, and you be grinning—for me there's no poetry like spoken Black poetry. When you experience a good Black poetry performance, the audience actually becomes a *congregation* joining in a quasi-religious cultural experience. I identified with that collective emotional experience, and I didn't know poetry could attain that. I thought poetry was read alone: very intellectual, very far removed from emotional involvement, and totally devoid of a collective experience. I thought I did not like poetry.

Mrs. Nelson changed that.

She dipped me deep beneath the waters by simply laying Langston Hughes on me. I received the word not from a book, not from my reading Hughes, but rather from hearing him, and hearing him with music, jazz, no less, and blues.

"Put your books away. I want you to listen to something."

I was not prepared for the Langston Hughes recording because if this was poetry, then poetry was me.

Until that moment, I had a disdain for "poetry." Given the total psychological schema of segregated America, my dilemma was but a minor example of the schizophrenia that marks the Negro's being.

As I became conscious—or, as we often say, as I "woke up"—and tried to figure a lot of this out, I was confounded. In my ignorance, I came up with some awfully dumb theories. I didn't know that all people had poetry, just had different ways of expressing it. Most of all I didn't know that, given who I was, there were ways of poetic expression that I preferred to others.

Although I had been taught and had absorbed certain lessons, I didn't *consciously* understand my people and my culture. Yes, I was Black. I could feel my culture and be moved by my culture, but feeling is not knowing. It is not enough to experience; we must also understand, if we are to become subjects, and not just objects, of culture and history.

Not only was I ignorant of myself, but even worse, I did not know that there was such a thing for Black people as "knowing thyself." In school when I read Shakespeare's words "to thine own self be true," I thought it profound. What was truly profound is that I didn't know that "know thyself" is a maxim found on the temple walls of ancient Egypt and in the folk tales of West Africa—indeed, found around the world.

For me, and most Black people, the very process of traditional mainstream education is alienating and engenders a psychological sense of both individual and racial inadequacy. That's why I had not ascribed philosophy, or poetry, to Black people even though it was all there. I was not only truly ignorant; I was the perfect product of America's educational system, which confuses Black people by rewarding those Blacks who evidence that they can "think" like Whites and who have an "understanding" of White culture, and fails those who do not evidence receptivity to and absorption of mainstream pedagogy regardless of what else that person knows and can do.

Fortunately for me and my junior high school peers, Mrs. Nelson knew something her students didn't know: Mrs. Nelson knew we young Blacks needed to be put in touch with ourselves. She knew we needed intellectual self-empowerment that didn't reference Europeans and American Whites as the paragons of culture, beauty, excellence and achievement. I recognize now that this self-pride, or "race consciousness," was not accidental in my development. Nevertheless, at the time I wasn't thinking about philosophical questions of self-esteem. I was thirteen.

I attended Rivers Frederick Junior High School, a public school named for a New Orleans physician of color. Because my mother was an elementary school teacher, I had not gone to a neighborhood school but rather went across town to the schools where she taught: first, Fisk Elementary for kindergarten through fourth. For fifth and sixth grades, I attended Phillis Wheatley (named for one of the first published African American poets, whose work I think of as a perfect example of Negro schizophrenia). Then I was sent to Frederick because at that time my parents judged Frederick the best of the Black public junior high schools.

Frederick more than lived up to its reputation. My first year there I got into photography via Mr. Conrad, the industrial arts teacher who set up a small darkroom in the industrial arts shop and started an after-school photography club. There were only about a half dozen of us who regularly participated. The impact of that experience has lasted throughout my life. After buying my first Yashica twin-lens reflex camera in seventh grade, there has never been a time when I did not own a camera.

Up until the time I got deep, deep into performance poetry and drama via the Free Southern Theatre, photography was a major, and more often than not "the" major, form of self-expression for me. At Frederick I became so identified with photography that many of my classmates referred to me as "the picture man."

Mr. Conrad taught photography as an avocation and as a social development mission. He probably received little, if any, school funding, and for certain he supplemented our shortfalls in the money to buy cameras, film, paper and chemicals with funds out of his own pocket. (Likewise, I'm sure, Mrs. Nelson had purchased that Langston Hughes record with her own funds.)

My three years at Frederick were a cultural breakthrough for me. I learned myself in a conscious way that was a culmination of all that had come before via my parents and my years in my grandfather's church. This was also a fitting prelude (and perhaps a critical spur) to my involvement in the civil rights movement and my conscious break with Creole and European goals and orientations.

I became conscious of myself as a positive and culturally active human being: I formed friendships that lasted far longer than those created in any other period of my formal education; I got involved in artistic self-expression; I experienced puppy love and first kissed girls; became conscious of the blues and of jazz; realized that there were languages other than English and began to learn French; traveled by myself for the first time to and from school; went out for the school football team (I didn't make it but found out later that even the coach who told me I "didn't have to come back" to practice expected me to show up the next day); fractured my leg playing sandlot football; became conscious of the petit bourgeoisie and the mind-set of Catholics; met kids who didn't simply pass for White but who, as the sons and daughters of doctors and lawyers, educators and business people, actually acted White; made decisions about how to spend my time after school; and, all in all, had a ball growing up through what is generally the most tempestuous period in the coming of age saga.

In short, at Frederick I became myself. Conscious self-development spared me the maiming conceptualization of myself as an intellectually and psychologically inferior victim of racism in America.

two: what Langston did

> *...I think that music, being an expression of the human heart, or of the human being itself, does express just what is happening. I feel it expresses the whole thing—the whole of human experience at the particular time that it is being expressed...I think music is an instrument. It can create the initial thought patterns that can change the thinking of the people.*
>
> *—John William Coltrane*

I know the exact moment I was saved as a writer: it was when I heard Langston Hughes reading his poetry with a jazz piano player in the background—all praises due Mrs. Nelson. I have since searched for but never found that record. Today I realize the record itself is of small consequence because, as is usually the case with such events, the memory is more potent than the reality.

After school I went straight to the main public library on Tulane Ave. Over the following weeks, I checked out everything I could find by Langston Hughes. I remember now and was absolutely astonished then by the concluding line of a poem about the death of a poor man in Harlem: "a poor man ain't got no business to die." I was as absorbed with Langston Hughes as a crib-bound baby playing with its own newly discovered hands and feet.

Being both ignorant and smitten, I made Hughes my measuring rod. For years, I thought to be a writer meant to be like Langston Hughes: meant to work and work hard at it; meant to write in every genre and to produce anthologies as well as individual books; meant to travel and communicate with people around the world; meant to do both journalism and creative writing; meant to celebrate the humanity of the planet through a focus on one's own folk. This is what I thought being a writer meant.

I never thought of being just a poet or just a journalist, just a dramatist or just an essayist. I never thought that writing one's own books was more important than editing and assembling the works of others. Tutored by Hughes, I quickly learned that people of color were writers and had a valuable literature.

Because I was inspired by the recording, I of course examined Hughes's poetry first—I remember reading an early, if not first, edition of *The Weary Blues* and some of Hughes's other early books, which had those beautiful etchings by E. McKnight Kauffer used as illustrations. To this day, I think poetry books ought to have pictures in them or at least artwork on the cover and not commercial graphics.

Oddly enough, while Langston's poetry deeply affected me, I moved quickly past what I initially thought was its stylistic simplicity. Of course, as I started trying to write, I found out that Langston's style was far from simple to duplicate.

Here are two of my early attempts, written, as near I can remember, sometime between 1963 and 1965. Both reflect the Langston Hughes influence and a definite use of blues. The second piece also evidences my interest in fantasy, or exaggeration, as a poetic technique.

2 SISTERS
STREET CORNER
CONVERSA(OBSERVA)TIONS
OTHER TALK THAN WHAT YOU HEAR

#

What
I got
Ain't for SALE

#

what ails a woman
worst than any pain
is to fall in love
with another woman man

#

my boss he white
I swear he do not know
where his hands belong

#

whiteman tell me
the rent is due
like the 15th
don't come every month

#

Ain't no hope
He be home soon
He got paid today

#

that child lord,
that baby got her daddy's eyes
& my husband's ways

#

O hum let me go

expected you yesterday

expected you yesterday & here you come today
a head full of pretty face & no excuses
about not coming till you came &
smiling from here to me
you know I gotta like the way you look
& the talk you puttin down
you're just taking advantage of me
you know I was going to wait
here have a star
what about a moon
do you like sky
the clouds are especially delicious
i ah...i ah
expected you yesterday & here you come today
a head full of pretty face & no excuses

I was writing poetry heavily influenced by Hughes's style rather than his poetry per se; Langston's autobiographies were his most important books for me, followed by the poetry anthologies he edited (particularly the collection of African poets). Another very influential Hughes book was *The Sweet Flypaper Of Life*, a photo/text collaboration with photographer Roy DeCavara. *Flypaper* set a photo essay standard, approached only by Amiri Baraka's book with Fundi (Billy Abernathy), *In Our Terribleness.*

The autobiographies were important because they served as road map; every writer Hughes mentioned, Black, White, African, Russian or Chinese, I went to the library and checked out a book. Some of the writers I liked, some I didn't.

Hughes was one side in the triangle of my conscious self-development. My civil rights involvement, picketing and sitting-in, was the second side. My interest in blues and jazz, which I pursued with a passionate intensity, completed the triangle.

I can remember all kinds of random specifics, such as joining the RCA record club and gradually getting to jazz through both White and Black artists. Before appreciating Duke Ellington and Ray Charles, I had a Chet Atkins record that had one Black-oriented cut on it, "Boo Boo Stick Beat." Chet Atkins was not a jazz artist, but at that time what did I know.

By the end of ninth grade, I had read my way through the Harlem Renaissance. I knew there were poets in Africa and the Caribbean. In high school, I started reading Turgenev and a little Pushkin, moved on to Chinese and Japanese writers, and generally found an alternative to Euro-centric classics as the touchstones of great literature. Thanks to Langston Hughes, once I started reading literature on my own, I never had an inferiority complex about it. I never thought that anyone White was necessarily the greatest writer I'd ever read or that I would not succeed until I could write like White writers or be like them.

I remember sitting in Mrs. Chavis's English class in ninth grade. We called her "say it and don't spray it" Mrs. Chavis because in her effort to enunciate clearly and to speak proper English, there was an exaggeration that often led to flying spittle. Here was the major deformity of petit bourgeois, aping White ways to the point of absurd caricature.

I dug Mrs. Nelson, who moved us deeper into ourselves, and I abhorred Mrs. Chavis, who had us chasing a white chalice, a chase that invariably included all kinds of soul-killing perversions and behavior entirely inappropriate for Black mental health.

Although I moved past Hughes stylistically, I never moved past Hughes' sensibility and his approach. Hughes kept working class Black folk as the central focus and foundation ground for all of his musings and philosophying. Since Hughes was ground zero for me. Nobody could influence me to abandon a Black focus.

At the same time, early on I got into some of the socially relevant and experimental non-Black writers. John Dos Passos and e.e. cummings come immediately to mind, but also the Beats and a lot of left-oriented literature from the thirties and forties. In these writers, I saw alternatives to almost everything that was in our textbooks. I did try to read the classic English poets, but they didn't hold me, as did few of the mainstream American poets, Carl Sandburg being an immediate exception.

This was the early sixties; an explosive proliferation of independence movements was happening on "the" continent and, indeed, throughout the Third World with an accompanying movement in literature. Langston Hughes had introduced me to much of this literature. There was also our domestic liberation movement, the civil rights movement, with its church base and freedom songs.

I believe for any writer to create a literature of value, one's work must necessarily be culturally specific, whether that culture be native or adopted. Hughes's folksy, blues orientation was more than culturally specific. What was most important to me was Hughes's resistance to assimilation, voiced through a celebration of and insistence on the nobility of our race. Of the African American writers I knew at that time, only Zora Neale Hurston approached Hughes in that wonderful and essential celebration and insistence.

"I'm like that old mule -- / Black -- and don't give a damn!/ You got to take me / Like I am." sang Hughes in one of his most popular poems. I liked that he saw nobility in the stubbornness of a mule, a stubborn insistence that is often ostracized as stupidity. Hughes knew who he was and presented himself without thoroughbred pretense, and for me, a young, Black male racing into adulthood via involvement in the civil rights movement, Hughes's mule was a touchstone I would continue to rub all the rest of my life.

This appreciation of one's people is not simply an intellectual activity. In America one does not love Black people simply because one is Black. In fact, in America one cannot love Black people simply on the basis of being. We must be taught both by instruction and by example to both bond with as well as identify with those who are the most despised, the most exploited, the most misused people in America. The trick, if one is Black, is to do this without developing a victim mentality of either self-hatred or self-pity and, at the same time, to avoid the temptation of overcompensation in the form of reversing the polarity of raw racism and declaring everything Black good and everything White evil. This is a very difficult task to master, even moreso in a public arena. It has never been easy for Black people to love themselves.

I was extremely blessed to experience the Civil Rights movement because this helped me to learn to love Black folk. When I was sixteen, I spent many Saturdays going door to door doing voter registration and voter education work. At that time, in order to register you had to fill out an arcane form that, among other bizarre hurdles, required an applicant to figure out her age exactly to the day. My job was both to convince people to register and to teach them how to correctly fill out the application.

While we often worked in the poorest neighborhoods of the city, I was culturally enriched because all of the houses I entered viscerally taught me aspects about my people and myself that I had not previously known, particularly the blues. While I taught neighbors mathematics, grammar and spelling, they taught me a music that literally wailed its defiance of status quo propriety.

There is nothing as defiant as the blues ten a.m. on Saturday morning, cranked up loud and reverberated by the wood of those row on row of sparely painted, if painted at all, shotgun houses.

Blues as tough as that woman who answered her door in a bra and brown skirt, cigarette at an angle in her mouth, an angle that complemented the comb in her hair. She continued combing her hair as I tried to convince her to register to vote, neither smiling nor scowling at my naive attempts to bring about what I thought would be an improvement in her life.

Twenty years later, reality supports this woman's stoicism in the face of my misplaced enthusiasm: the granddaughter of that woman is locked in an even deeper funk after generations of Black elected officials have presided over a worsening of social conditions for her and all the people like her. This woman standing before me knows that I'm a fool to think that registering to vote will change her life for the better. Yet, like Black women have for centuries in America, she balances the bubble of my foolish vision with a resigned and sophisticated agreement to buoy the dreams of a Black man—regardless of the certainty that his dream will never come true.

Black women somehow "know" that a man cannot live without dreams, realizable or not, so they identify not with our perennially deferred dreams, but rather they identify with us, the dreamers. This agreement is not with abstract ideals but rather with the flesh, blood and soul vision of our manhood.

That is why there is a man moving to the back of the house as I enter the door, a man who does not even want to discuss voting; a man who does not belong to this house and who probably does little to support this house; a man that this woman lets into her life without any great expectations just like she allows me to enter her living room, her house, her life, without any great expectations.

I am looking at her breasts. She watches me, does not blush, and why should she? She probably assumes that if I have not seen breasts before, then now is as good a time as any for me to begin looking. I slowly explain the procedures as we sit on an old sofa, or on beat up old kitchen chairs, or, I don't remember what we sat on. I don't remember anything except that inside that house was a whole world, a different world from the church-bred houses I usually inhabited. The difference was not the people but rather the way the people lived: the smells, the liquor, the absence of White gods on the wall (there were no pictures of Jesus or Kennedy in those houses), and, above all, the mule sound of the blues bleating in all its immutable Blackness.

In that house lived a blues so stark that when she raises her arm there is hair in her armpit, and she still has not bothered to put on a blouse. By the time we are going through the questions, I find her smiling as I explain that there are some simple tricks she can use to get through this thing. Soon we are both comfortable with each other, and a half hour later I exit back onto the streets with a notation of her name and address so that we can follow-up on whether she registers.

Her arm reaches out to close the door, which sometimes has a shutter that opens out, and, even as the shutter closes, the blues continues to blow. Now she is smiling and maybe calls me "baby" with the conspiratorial smile that Black women fleetingly flash after pumping up a Black male ego, the smile that plants seeds designed to strengthen the recipient who must face a world designed to grind Black people down. The incubation period sometimes takes years, but eventually I realize who was really helping whom. Blues like that.

Nothing stops the blues because the blues was created precisely as a way to overcome. This is how I come to realize the power of the blues, the power is like that woman being herself and facing life just as it is and just as she is, and still believing in a naive high schooler knocking on her door.

This woman, with the blues as her song, survives an unconditional confrontation with life. She taught me exactly what Langston meant by "just like I am." We didn't need to clean up. We didn't need to talk differently. We didn't even need to wear socially acceptable clothes. And we didn't need to stop shouting the blues. If they wanted us: take us like we were. If we wanted to change, that was our choice rather than some alien requirement of life. Blues like that is what I learned going door to door throughout the community.

The blues remains self-referential, always grounded in the here and now. Some people think the blues is about submission because the blues is reality based and embraces the world as it is while at the same time wishing for, indeed longing for, the world to be different. The Christian worldview, on the other hand, is viewed as "uplifting" even though it is other-referential, about life in the hereafter, based on faith in things unseen and a general exclusion of anyone who is not also Christian, despite Christianity's philosophical support of being good Samaritans and doing unto others.

When I did my civil rights canvassing, I experienced the deep blues and found myself drawn to and responding to a side of my birthright that theretofore I had only read about in Langston Hughes and Zora Neale Hurston's work and had only recently begun to listen to on records. Until then I had never really heard the blues, even though the blues was in my blood.

As I canvassed and listened to the music and listened to the people talk, and as I tried to make them comfortable while giving my spiel about registering; as we walked the picket lines outside the department stores and talked to people, trying to persuade them not to shop; all of that not only put me in contact with working class Black people, but more importantly, those experiences put me in contact with more of myself.

Regardless of whether these people thought what I was about was important, it was my job to convince them of the importance of what I was trying to get them to do, and in the process, I began to understand that I was "them," and it was "we" who were important.

Once I accepted that what my people did or didn't do was important, then I could never look down on them, nor could I think that what happened to me personally was the only important part of life. I never felt that because I could read, write and figure I was somehow better off. Although I went to school with the sons of doctors, lawyers and civil servants at St. Aug, because of the civil rights movement, I identified more with the laborers than with the professionals, and I firmly believed that I could be of service to them.

This identification, furthermore, was consciously constructed because I not only learned from watching and working with people in the civil rights movement, I also started studying the blues: reading books about the blues and buying blues records and the same with jazz. I had the world of gospel in my upbringing, but I came to the blues as someone who did not move through the blues world on a day to day basis, and, aware of my distance, I closed the gap through study and through civil rights work.

I got the best of both worlds, my upbringing grounding me in a Christian community of caring folk and my civil rights work and junior high school education grounding me in intimate contact with blues folk. Again, I point to Hughes as a guide.

I loved Hughes's poem "Motto" which ended with: "My motto, / As I live and learn, / is: / Dig And Be Dug / In Return." Dig. Hughes said nothing specific about what to dig, so implicitly, at least to my way of thinking, that "dig" meant "dig" the world. In fact, in the opening stanza Hughes says: "I play it cool / And dig all jive. / That's the reason / I stay alive." This is Hughes's great attraction for me: he told me to be myself, and he told me to dig the world. Yes, and that's deep.

After Hughes, only Baldwin and Baraka significantly and permanently influenced my writing style. All three of them engaged the world with both an outsider's critical eye and a grounded Black person's love of Black folk.

I found Baldwin technically awesome. I can remember reading some essay he wrote with the word "proffer" in it, which became a word I used in my own writings. Critics often credit Baldwin's use of language to the Bible, but really it's not the Bible per se; it's the Bible mediated through the Black church, and it's also jazz, the complex outpourings of bebop. Look at the sentence structures, the very volubility of his sentences; everything and the kitchen sink pushed against each other in breathless rushes of prose. Baldwin's denseness was balanced by an unerring rhythmic logic that made his fanciful prose flights a joy to read.

When Baldwin took America to task, as he did so eloquently in his play *Blues For Mr. Charlie* and in his famous essay "The Fire Next Time," he did it with the same stylistic brilliance evidenced by the creators of bebop. Baldwin's best prose had not only the Old Testament fire and brimstone, raunchy forthrightness and righteous indignation, but that prose also advanced the art of the essay as a genre. Baldwin was much like Charlie Parker and Dizzy Gillespie, who ushered in a whole new musical style, a style that, at its core, had the grandiose, stubbornly elegant simplicity of Thelonious Monk articulating stark truths in a uniquely offbeat manner, a manner that both demanded an audience and made demands of its audience with the same explosive pronouncements as the drumming of Max Roach and Kenny "Klook" Clarke elevating rhythm to new heights.

I know that Baldwin loved gospel and blues, but he also loved jazz—so many of his major characters were musicians and lovers of music/musicians. Mary Ellison in her book *Extensions of the Blues* references a Baldwin quote from biographer Fern M. Eckman's book *The Furious Passage of James Baldwin*: "When Baldwin was a keynote speaker at a conference on 'The Negro Writer's Vision of America' in the early sixties, he declared 'My models—my private models—are not Hemingway, nor Faulkner, nor Dos Passos, or indeed any American writer. I model myself on jazz musicians, dancers, a couple of whores and a few junkies...'" If you don't understand the music, then you will be blind to the music's influence on Baldwin.

In 1964, my senior year at St. Augustine High School, praising Baldwin got me kicked off the student newspaper. St. Aug's major reputation was as our city's premier college prep school for

Black males. It is no accident that many of my former classmates have gone on to become Black professionals. Further, it is no accident that many of the managers of city government post 1973 are alumni of Catholic schools in general and St. Aug specifically. By the time I was sent there, psychologically I was in total conflict with their mainstream American cultural orientation.

Back in eighth grade at Frederick, after being introduced to Hughes, I joined the school newspaper. Mrs. Nelson was the advisor. I was writing and doing photography, and eventually I became the editor. We entered the paper in a contest sponsored by Columbia University in New York and won second place. Us. A little Negro junior high school paper. Winning made me know I was a match for the world, for the best of America.

At St. Aug I wanted to continue with my journalism. I wrote a glowing review of Baldwin's incendiary "Blues For Mr. Charlie," which, while not rejecting religion, ended by espousing self-defense, picking up the gun.

The priests said not in this paper, not at this school, not in this life. I realized we were in direct conflict with each other. They wanted me to study and make straight A's. They wanted me to give up or tone down my civil rights work. One teacher, Fr. McManus, who was a "liberal" on the Urban League board and all that, went completely out of his tree when he walked into homeroom, and I was sitting there reading *Muhammad Speaks*. I had no idea it would provoke him to turn redder than a redneck sheriff watching Sidney Portier in *Guess Who's Coming To Dinner*.

Fr. Mac, who was known for his prowess at corporal punishment with the paddle, stomped the floor, bellowed at me, and over the next month took every opportunity to remind me that I would be better off studying than reading that crap. I laughed and wondered what was so threatening. They knew I was dangerous before I knew.

And there was the time an English teacher told me that I was going to write a term paper on fancy, fantasy and some other "f" word in one of Shakespeare's sonnets. I immediately said I wasn't going to do it. "Well, if you don't do it, Ferdinand, you're just going to get an F for the semester."

"You can just give me my F now because I'm not going to do it."

I went home that evening and told my mother that I was going to get an F. Neither she nor my father forced me to return to school and apologize, or even to write the assignment. They let me happily hold onto both my F and my budding sense of rebellion and dignity.

Years and years later when my children were going through school, I never ever sided with the school when any of the children rebelled. I made sure that the children understood that there were repercussions they would have to bear as a result of their actions, but the larger picture for me was that I refused to repress rebellion in the youth. Indeed, not only did I want to encourage that rebellion because I knew ultimately it was healthy, but also, I recognized that the whole system was set up to smother our rebellious spirits. Why should I help the system to maintain the status quo?

As a parent, I made a conscious decision. As a high school student, I intuitively concluded that St. Aug's discipline was a conscious attempt to season a slave.

Sometimes we exaggerate the severity of a situation because memory is selective, and everyone wants to tell a good tale about themselves, but there were too many incidents at St. Aug to ignore. For example, I once went out for the drama club when they were doing some English drawing room comedy with fake British accents, butlers and dry jokes. In eighth grade at Frederick, I had played Crispus Attucks in my civic teacher's drama. Under Mrs. Green's direction, my big scene was to leap out of the closet with a sword made of a clothes hanger and cardboard and confront the British soldiers with the declaratory line: "I am a desperate Black man who is willing to fight for my freedom."

So, you know I thought St. Aug's British bullshit was just that, i.e., British bullshit. I quit after attending one rehearsal.

At Frederick they armed me. At St. Aug they tried to castrate me.

Most of my teachers at Frederick had been significant Black women with an important handful of bold Black men, such as Mr. Conrad, Mr. Howard, who taught me French, and Mr. Blanchard, who gave me a love for mathematics. At St. Aug the instructors were mainly priests (who were mostly White) of the Josephite Order. The Josephites were an order that focused on educating Black people. Most of the lay instructors at St. Aug were pious, intellectually oriented Black men who at the time struck me as effeminate. The dichotomy between the instructors at the two schools was too ludicrous for words. I owed St. Aug nothing except my muleish contempt.

All of this time I am still reading and still struggling to write. By twelfth grade I finish an experimental novel that ends with the hero committing suicide. No matter how much I thought I was uninfluenced by St. Aug, no matter how much I fought against their example and instructions, still, I obviously was ingesting some of their messages, especially the message to become respectable by killing the Black blues self.

Baldwin's writings spoke directly to me because here I was confronting a sensibility, a system whose total intent was to turn the blues-based Black into a Christian American. In St. Aug's schema, similar to Mrs. Chavis's, integration meant effacing one's self. They taught young Black males that the highest achievement for Blacks was to speak, dress, conduct oneself and be around Whites as though we were not who we were. Ultimately, they wanted to put into our hearts the desire to be like Whites and into our heads the belief that being like Whites equated with being intelligent, civilized and Christian.

My acceptance of such a mainstream scenario inevitably would have meant submerging every conflict, sucking contradictions up and in, and contorting my psyche just to be acceptable. I resisted and stayed in constant rebellion.

In that context, Baldwin's penetrating intelligence appealed to me because his example allowed me to confront the status quo norms in their own arena. Baldwin's use of language and mastery of the essay signified not only his ability to handle White words but also his ability to bend those words for his own use. Initially, that appealed to me.

Had I stopped there I would have been forever trapped, because ultimately, striving to express one's self solely by mastering the master's language presupposes that language is value-free, that language is neutral, and somehow, even though I did not "know" in a theoretical sense that language was the articulation of culture, emotionally moved by Black music, I did feel that I needed my own language. The Catholic rejection of gospel and blues was a confirmation of Black music's importance. Reading Baldwin, beneath his mastery of the "King's" English, I heard, and felt, a love of Black music.

In later years Baldwin addressed the issue of language in his own eloquent way, noting that "Black English" was essentially a language and ought to be respected as such. While Baldwin was not the only person to address this issue, what distinguished Baldwin's contribution was his emphasis on the necessity of language. Baldwin's penetration to the sine qua non of this issue reinforced in me the necessity of articulating what we had been doing with language. But here I am jumping ahead of myself. Back then all I knew was that it felt right to speak, write and listen to the language(s) I loved and understood.

Needless to say, the blues with its confrontation of pain appealed to me. Although I was unable to avoid both the positive and the negative influences—the Latin and English, the religion classes and the skewed history, the emphasis on getting high marks on the SAT and IQ tests, the uniform of wearing a tie every school day and the insistence on proper English spoken at all times—even as all of that was influencing me, fortunately, there was the counterweight of the literature I was reading, the music I was listening to and studying, and above all, the civil rights movement within which I was deeply and actively immersed. In Baldwin I found a companion who championed all that I found valuable.

After Baldwin came Leroi Jones/Amiri Baraka. Baraka I dug because of his iconoclastic and boldly innovative stylings. He is always at his best breaking ground, making you go "damn" at the way he has hooked something up with the sarcastic aloofness of a hard bop hipster. Clearly, as the quantity and quality of his earliest work demonstrates, Baraka worked hard at being off the cuff. Like a great jazz musician, he had sheded (i.e., "woodshed," jazz parlance for practice and serious study) heavy so that whenever the time came to blow, he was able to blow with confidence and make his work sound effortless. Baraka also projected a cocky air of being ahead of the curve, always in the know, always the first one to arrive on the set wondering what took the rest of us so long to arrive. That appealed to the machismo in my adolescent male psyche.

But what most appealed to me was that Jones too was struggling in the White world, struggling to define and claim his persona as a Black man. Additionally, Jones was deep into the music, especially jazz and blues. Through Jones I also started to experience poetry as self-revelation.

Jones's own personal life experiences, conundrums, confusions, dreams and aspirations were at the center of his poetry. On the stylistic surface, Jones's poetry was nothing like Hughes's, but yet, underneath it, there was a deep blues, a blues for the lost Black man, the man unsure of what being himself meant, the "dead lecturer." That title of Jones's second book of poetry said it all.

A lot of Jones I didn't understand, couldn't understand, and even if I had understood, it never would have been something I could've really related to. But what attracted me, I think, to Jones before he became Baraka, as well as what attracted me to Baldwin, was the way he confronted the White world and also confronted his complicity and love of that world; the way he articulated and embraced with critical consciousness his love of White literature, which directly correlated with my own less ambivalent, but not totally uncontradictory, feelings about what I was learning in school. Much of what both Jones and Baldwin spoke about along these lines resonated in my experience.

Anyone who has not experienced it will find it nearly impossible to understand the schizophrenia that mainstream education engenders in working class Black people, right down to the root of rejecting one's mother, which is the embodiment of rejecting one's culture. This is why Black studies was so immediately latched onto by students and so instantly rejected by the petit bourgeois-oriented colored professors and why Afrocentrism is often strongest in predominantly White institutions of higher education. At no other time in one's life will the intellectual challenge to and intellectual oppression of Black people be as clear as when you are a Black student in a predominately White school, precisely because in higher education there are few, if any, status quo-revered Black intellectual authority figures—and of those there are, almost all are either conservative or seemingly apolitical.

On the other hand, there is no way for a sane person to reject learning, to reject intelligence. I wanted to embrace my people, embrace myself and the world I grew up in, but there was a conflict within that world. The wannabes stumbling and fleeing toward the status quo invariably would put down the blues folk, put down their ignorance, their uncouthness, their illiteracy, their blues essence. In what the wannabes perceived as a rejection of intellectual values, rather than a rejection of self-abnegating intellectualism, blues people seemed to be so short sighted, so self-destructive and so incorrigible.

Hughes did not speak to this conflict as cogently nor as consistently as Baldwin and Jones/Baraka did. There is a detachment in Hughes's writing that maintains the privacy of the witness even as Hughes focuses almost exclusively on his people. Baldwin and Baraka, on the other hand, with Whites intimately involved in their lives, focus much more on the contradictions of being a Black man in White America as a personal rather than an observed experience.

Hughes's reticence about his personal life eventually became an alienating factor for me. Hughes had written two autobiographies, and by the early sixties, neither Baldwin nor Baraka had written any, yet readers knew more about each of their personal lives than about Hughes's personal life. This is a line of demarcation. In later years, I would develop my theory about the use of the "personal," but at that time I simply did the most expedient thing: I loved both approaches, the detachment of Hughes and the personal involvement of Baldwin/Baraka.

Baldwin and Baraka wrote in a modern intellectual style and that appealed to me. Yet, neither Baldwin nor Baraka had that element of blues-based holisticness that was the most marvelous quality of Langston Hughes, a writer so huge that his collected works define literature. Hughes was a "simple" Black writer who went around the world.

To an adolescent eighth grader in 1959/60 just waking up to literature, Hughes was a blessing and a foundation. After Hughes, nothing was too deep to tackle. Hughes gave me a sense of self-confidence as a budding Black writer. Before I realized that there was such a thing as a literary ghetto, I was already literally looking at the entire world.

three: I choose to be a writer

> *Well, I tell you for myself, I make a conscious attempt, I think I can truthfully say that in music I make or I have tried to make a conscious attempt to change what I've found, in music. In other words, I've tried to say, 'Well, this I feel, could be better, in my opinion, so I will try to do this to make it better.' This is what I feel that we feel in any situation that we find in our lives, when there's something we think could be better, we must make an effort to try and make it better. So it's the same socially, musically, politically, and in any department of our lives.*
>
> *—John William Coltrane*

I was slow to commit to writing. When I graduated from high school in 1964, photography was my first love and music my deepest passion. After graduation, I went on an eleven-year odyssey in and out of higher education that culminated in a business administration associate arts degree from Delgado Vocational-Technical Junior College in 1975.

I have never liked college. From a pedagogical standpoint, I perceived it as an extension of high school. Nevertheless, there is no denying the importance of many of the experiences I had in colleges.

First, I was one of eleven "American Negroes" at Carleton College in Northfield, Minnesota—the mythic site of one of Jesse James's last and most disastrous attempts at bank robbery. St. Aug's reputation led to Carleton offering me a partial scholarship.

In addition to musicians such as drummer Art Blakey and Ravi Shankar, at Carleton I was able to see and meet a variety of influential people, such as socialist Norman Thomas and members of the budding White leftist organization Students for a Democratic Society (SDS). I became a radio programmer with my own jazz show on the college station. Also important for me was the opportunity to meet and talk with students from Africa and other foreign places. Carleton exposed me to an enormous amount of foreign cinema, and I have been an avid cinema buff since.

Through an improbable twist of circumstances, I even got to meet writer John Oliver Killens, whose World War II novel *And Then We Heard The Thunder* was, during that period, my favorite piece of fiction. Carleton started an exchange program with the historically important Black school Fisk University in Nashville, Tennessee. In their attempts to keep me from applying, Carleton's administrators informed me that the program was designed to send *White* students to Fisk in exchange for accepting Black students at Carleton. I reminded them that the program guidelines said nothing about the race of students, beyond the administration's idea of who could better benefit from comparing the two schools.

While I was at Fisk, I went to a writing workshop conducted by John Killens. Years later, Killens chose to include my work in an anthology of Black southern writers that was posthumously completed by my friend Dr. Jerry Ward of Tougaloo College in Mississippi after Mr. Killens died.

During this period, I also developed a relationship with Esim Bozoklar, a young student from Turkey. She inspired me to write a series of numbered poems called, as best I can recall, "*mavi gok*," which was Turkish for "blue sky."

The major benefit of going to Carleton, however, was that the experience forced me to examine myself in a setting even more challenging than St. Aug—and by the end of the second trimester, I was predictably confused. Ultimately Carleton was a great and expensive learning experience that I quickly rejected. By the time I left, I had written, in addition to a lot of poetry, a second novel revolving around a desperate group of young Blacks at a predominantly White college.

Overall, my poetic influences at that time were Hughes for content and e.e.cummings for visual presentation (the breaking of words into letters and the explosion of one word erupting from another word or interrupting the word flow). Although I've lost most of my work from this era, here are two poems which exemplify both my state of mind and some of the cummings influence.

no entrance

the vo
ice might
y voice
of Go
d visit
ed me la
st ni
te it sa
id “fuc
k you” &
so I tu
rned ov
er on m
y stomac
h that i
t might be
easier/not
that He ne
eded it -
He was real
ly doing su
ch a go
od job al
ready!

[untitled]

those good things there be that are
are more surely killers more deadly lethal
than any evil be
for sometimes even dreams become
poisonous & aspirations abortions of life
sometimes the very hope amputates
sometimes the better worsens
it is not the envisioning of dreams nor
the rise toward aspirations
only the survival midst this all
that can keep us
it sometimes matters not that you fail only
that you've survived it
somehow is the resurrection more cherished than the climb

to be the phoenix more surely is harder than ever the god to be
more straight more true
than any glory ever

When I quit Carleton, I returned to New Orleans and literally surrendered to the army. It was 1965, the height of the Vietnam draft. I had turned 18 but had not registered. Finally, as a result of my mother's insistence, I went down to the draft board. I can still hear this elderly White woman shrieking about how I had broken the law, could go to jail, and had better report there the next day at noon. I don't volunteer for executions, so I went to the recruiting offices downtown and volunteered to go anywhere but Vietnam. The recruiter said he couldn't promise to send me to a particular place, but if I did well on a battery of tests, he would get me into a "mos" (occupational service area) that they didn't use in Vietnam.

I never returned to the draft board and in fact didn't receive my draft card until after I was in boot camp at Fort Polk, Louisiana. I ended up in electronic repair of the Nike Hercules nuclear missile, which meant a nine-month training period at Fort Bliss in El Paso, Texas. I served a year in Korea and finished out my army stint back at Ft. Bliss.

When I returned to Bliss, I was a sergeant and had lots of free time. I lived in the darkroom, the music practice room and the library, in that order. Because of my rank, I didn't have to make roll calls and also had my own room in the barracks. I would be the first at the USO, check out a set of drums, go into a practice room and practice playing drums for an hour before any of the other musician-soldiers arrived. After some months of intensive practice, I developed into an in-demand drummer. I played in a soul band, as well as in a rock trio as a sub when their regular drummer couldn't make it, and eventually in a small band which played both jazz & R&B.

By then the photography was mainly on the weekends, and I would go back to my room and write at night. I didn't read as much as I had in college, partly because the army library was predictably conservative. The three journals I read and subscribed to were *The Liberator* magazine, *Negro Digest*, and *The Village Voice*.

By 1968, my fiction had developed to the point that I was good enough to get a publisher strongly interested in my work. I had sent a set of short stories, *Easy Rider, Dark Rider*, to William and Morrow (because that's where LeRoi Jones was published) and to Dial (because of James Baldwin). Phil Petrie wrote me back encouraging me to send him more stories.

Easy Rider contains six stories comprising about seventy pages. The first five stories are written in the first person from the point of view of the protagonist. The last story is in the third person and makes a jump of about twenty years. I know now that Mr. Petrie was simply asking for at least one more story to bridge the chasm of years. Had I done that and the book had been successfully published, I may have chosen to pursue fiction rather than poetry as my main voice. As it was, in 1971 I had a story published in *Young Black Storytellers* edited by Orde Coombs, and in 1973 another story was published in *We Be Word Sorcerers* edited by Sonia Sanchez.

So, why didn't I continue fiction? The real answer is I don't really know. I suppose this is sort of like asking John Coltrane why didn't he continue to play alto rather than switch to tenor saxophone. Who knows?

I frequently tell people that fiction is the hardest form for me to write, but that's not entirely true. What is true is that there was an extremely limited number of Black publishing opportunities in the sixties—even though, on a national level, I was more successful with fiction than with poetry. After I got out of the army, except for anthologies, I had no desire to pursue publishing with mainstream companies and looked exclusively for Black outlets.

Even though I wrote two novels early on, the novel has never appealed to me as a professional writer. Short stories, yes, but the novel, no. I have theorized about the novel being a bourgeois, Euro-centric genre. I have made up off-the-wall arguments about fiction in general. But none of that addresses the central issue: for me, fiction lacks the oratorical element.

Both poetry and drama are recited, spoken aloud, or sung before an audience. I think those of us engaged in the Black aesthetic movement gravitate to the orated as opposed to the textual partly out of personal taste and partly because, as currently demonstrated by rap music, our community responds more forcefully to the orated than the textual. Given our community's "church" and "street corner" orientation, each of which places a high value on oratorical abilities, the preference for spoken over written text is natural, grows organically out of our environment.

Additionally, for us, text is like lyrics separated from music. One cannot appreciate rap at all if one never hears rap and only reads the text of a rap. On the other hand, even if you don't or can't understand every word that a rapper says, you still can appreciate and be moved by the rap once you hear it.

Of course, in early 1968, looking forward to getting out of the army, playing music professionally, and writing at night, I had not come to any of these conclusions. I was writing fiction constantly, and I was not writing that much poetry. I was a closet writer. My writing was so deep in the closet that I never hesitated to focus on my music at the expense of time spent writing. My writing was going nowhere but in a drawer, a box, a folder, a closet. But my music, that was another story.

By the time I mustered out of the army, our band had all kinds of gigs lined up, and we had become very popular. I promised my bandmates I would return after I visited my family for a week or so. "Yeah, I'm coming back. I'm leaving my drums here, and you know I'm not going to abandon my drums."

I never saw those drums again.

In New Orleans I heard drummers who made my fingers and hands deny ever, ever holding a drumstick. Those cats beat me into a serious inadequacy crisis. No matter how hard I practiced, I would never be able to play as well as they did. They nullified any aspirations I had to be a musician. I was too realistic to fool myself. On the one hand, I knew Zigaboo Modeliste of the Meters, Smokey Johnson of Fats Domino's Band, and David Lee, who eventually was snatched up by Dizzy Gillespie, plus "beaucoup" (a bunch, almost too many to count) other New Orleans drummers, could drum circles around me.

On the other hand, I didn't know or know of any New Orleanians who could write better than me.

Right then and there, I gave up music as a profession. I had not yet definitely decided to try writing as a profession. However, my realistic choices had been narrowed considerably. I did recognize, however, that writing, like music, would always be a part of my life.

More so than hearing Langston Hughes in eighth grade, more so than quitting college and going into the army, my decision not to pursue music as a profession, coupled with my strong desire to participate in the Black power struggle, defined the way ahead.

four. BLKARTSOUTH

> *...it seems to me that the audience, in listening, is in an act of participation, you know. And when you know that somebody is maybe moved the same way you are, to such a degree or approaching the degree, it's just like having another member in the group.*
>
> *—John William Coltrane*

Here it was, July 1968 and although I had rejected the profession of music and also was impelled toward participating in the Black power movement, other than a gradually cohering desire to write, I had absolutely no idea about what I wanted to do with my life.

Part of the problem was I really didn't know any writers personally, so I had no idea what the writing life was actually about or how to go about becoming a writer.

Unlike abandoning music, my decision to be a writer was not spurred by a specific incident or a specific realization. Over the next six months, I found myself writing more and more, and found the people around me responding to the poetry I was writing. So, after getting positive feedback, I just kept on doing it.

In September of 1968 I tried college again. I enrolled as a freshman at SUNO (Southern University in New Orleans). I ran headfirst into academe and its ignorance of and disdain for the black arts movement. I wrote a poem called "John Who" that focused on the overall ignorance of John Coltrane by various faculty members in the different departments. Then there was the incident that dimmed any hope of my reaching some detente with SUNO's administration.

I was in Dr. Taylor's English lit class. One of the American ballads we were studying was a blues ballad; I think it was "Frankie and Johnny," and there was the phrase: "the window was throwed up high." Dr. Taylor, who had her Ph.D. in Chaucer or some other area of "olde English," asked did anyone know what the phrase meant.

I smiled. That was easy. I told her it meant the window was wide open, "like in 'when you see me coming, throw yo window high, when you see me leaving, hang yo head and cry.'" She told me I was wrong. She said that what the phrase referred to was the architecture of the period and how the windows were built high off the ground. Well I didn't know architecture, but I did know bullshit.

On the other side of the coin, my writing was fueled in part by the impatience and arrogance of youth. Here is a short poem from that period. Imagine this piece read by a bushy headed, sunglass-wearing (we was so cool we sometimes even wore sunglasses at night) militant.

madpoet

the madpoet, mad, mad, mad
poet, the niggerpoet, the black
poet, mad, mad
how many black angels can dance on a watermelon seed
how many english teachers can fly
how many historians are white
how many records do J.B. sell for his white bosses
how many women wear wigs
how many women wear natural wigs
how many black folk vote for wallace
how many cadillacs parked in tenement lots
how many men do janitorial work in alligator shoes
how many men work
how many got alligator shoes
how many people think shelly pope is pretty
how many women with babies that look more like
    their man than their husbands
how many gods do christians believe, any
how many space ships the man gon build
how many rivers and lakes still fresh water
how many black students know how to read and write
how many black students go to school
how many schools do we have
how many colleges in the city are schools
how many so-called hip people is frontin
how many cigarettes you smoke
how many fifths can you drink
how many us think we together
how many us together

By the end of the first semester, I and a handful of other students, some of whom were veterans like myself, were in open rebellion against the administration. By the spring semester of 1969 we organized a takeover of the university, completely shutting it down. In New Orleans I became known as both a militant leader and the leader of a drama group; the two identities were often fused in the public's mind.

I used my poems at community events and various community programs where I was a volunteer. One of my first major pieces in that regard was "All In The Street," which spoke in poetic tones about the tidal wave of us dancing in the street with brass bands. The poem had the closing line that suggested, just like we took the streets, "the cities are next."

At this point I began experimenting with using New Orleans music in my work. It was conscious in that I knew I was doing it, but subconscious in that I had not figured out what I was doing other than emulating the music and/or being inspired by specific musical performances. As I developed, the music became more and more integral to both the structure and the performance of my poetry.

Here is where my basic style as a public poet got its start. I wanted to reflect and project the dreams and aspirations, the reality and history, the ethos and diverse ideologies of my community, a community on the move, in transition from oppression to liberation. Some view this simply as polemical poetry, but for me, a particular party line was not the important thing. The important thing was the identification with the community at large and the desire to serve my community.

My desire determined a style. My work had to be mass oriented. The images, the metaphors, the themes, the concerns and the emotional orientations, all had to draw on the social realities of our community, or else it would be rejected or, worse yet, ignored.

Audience is a major force in the style of any and every poet. Some poets never think of or define their audience. Some say that they write from the heart or write the truth and that whoever appreciates that work is the audience. But, even in those cases, is it not true that the language of the poetry will determine who is in a position to relate to (both understand and appreciate) the poetry both stylistically and content-wise?

A critical part of my style was the utilization of the oral as a poetic sine qua non. For me and my community, it was not enough for the poetry to exist as text. Our poetry also needed to be oral.

I remembered reading Langston Hughes' explanation of rhyme being more easily remembered by the poet, but especially also by the audience. I used rhyme but not necessarily at the ends of lines. Early on, I learned to use what I call internal rhymes and absolute rhymes. An internal rhyme was the use of the same and similar sounds in the middle of lines but rhythmically in the same place in different lines. An absolute rhyme was the repeating of the same word or phrase, usually at the beginning of the line but sometimes at the end.

In addition to rhyme, irony and humor (particularly sarcasm and caricature) were important elements of my early style precisely because community people responded to these elements. Irony—deliberate understatement and/or the emphasizing of the split between the literal meaning and the contextual meaning of a word, phrase, idea or image—is a hallmark of African American humor. Irony is also a mask, a tool for resistance and rebellion presented in a seemingly innocuous or nonthreatening manner. Finally, irony is reinterpretation by causing the audience to reconsider a given reality from a different point of view. Next to the use of music, irony is probably the salient characteristic of our work from that period.

Here is a poem, "Leader," which is illustrative of the period. This is actually a choreopoem in that it was both a dance and a poem. Eventually, we had a whole set of dance poems that we did like a chorus line with different members taking the lead. Similarly, we had a set of "hair" poems.

"Leader" opens with me clapping and improvising a funky dance while encouraging the audience to clap along, which usually didn't take much encouragement. At some point in the dance I would stop, move directly to the audience, recite the poem with a cocky air and at the conclusion go back to dancing.

Leader

i saw a Negro at a dance
last nite who called himself
my leader & that nigger
couldn't dance to save his life
so how he gon lead me!

That summer and fall of 1968, just out of the army, full of fire and engaged in community activity, I found the perfect stage for my calling as a community-based writer at the Free Southern Theatre. I went to both the weekly writing workshops conducted by Tom Dent and to the weekly drama workshops conducted by Robert "Big Daddy" Costley. There were only a handful of us attending either workshop with a core of three or four of us who attended both. Eventually the workshops combined, and that led to the development of the writing/performing workshop, which eventually developed its own identity as BLKARTSOUTH.

Excepting for Tom Dent, none of the other workshop members thought of writing in terms of fiction or prose. Much of what would normally have been channeled in that direction was redirected into drama and performance poetry partly because there was immediate feedback. Not only did we critique each other's work, we also would give the work dramatized readings.

Here are two of the first poems I published in *Nkombo*, our literary journal. Both of them are blues. "Love" is a traditional blues piece written under the influence of Langston Hughes, and "And Black women!" is a more modern blues, self-referential and intentionally didactic.

Love

less you ever been in love
you cannot understand
what I mean when I say
I love my baby so hard
it sometimes make me want to cry

(untitled)

And Black women!
the wet shining beauty
brown eyed and ebony hued
you mothers, sisters, wives, lovers all
we revere you, need you/build
stronger manhoods more worthy of you
than has been our fate to be in years
recent past, cowardly living like sheep
no longer, we rise with the noble
intentions of taking you into our
arms, into our homes, into
black families (...this propaganda of
words will sound strange to all who
do not know or realize the worth of
our beautiful black women) perhaps,
this poem can open the eyes of some
young Afro American to the beauty
of the black girl living in his
community; we have only to look with
our eyes & quit using a foreign
myopic blue eyed aesthetic and we will
see ourselves, and love ourselves

The late sixties and early seventies were a time when Black people literally were reciting poetry on street corners, on buses, in churches and temples, at rallies and demonstrations, in playgrounds and in gymnasiums. This was a time when poetry mattered and was vital, had meaning for everyone whether young or old, male or female, college educated or a high school drop-out. In that context, to be a community-respected poet was nothing short of being a messenger from the spirit world, a juju man/woman. To appreciate our theoretical approach to poetry, you must understand the context.

My first year in the workshop was the key to my decision to become a professional writer. I was developing a voice, and I had found a writing community—actually, I had helped create a writing community. From the beginning, I served as co-editor of *Nkombo*, and later when the workshop officially became BLKARTSOUTH, I became the director.

While I do not separate developing a voice from the development of the writing community, the truth is that other than Tom Dent, I had done more writing than anyone else in the workshop, and it was quickly apparent. At first, I was recycling stories and poems I had written while in the army as well as writing new material, but then I hit on writing a play entirely in verse. *BLK LOVE SONG #1* became one of my most successful plays on a national and international level, even though it never played as much as some of the other more conventional pieces I wrote, such as *The Picket* and *Mama* (which was our biggest hit).

While some of the other plays were more popular and had been performed throughout the South, they had not been published. In 1974, *BLK LOVE SONG* was selected for inclusion in the monumental work *Black Theater USA: 45 Plays By Black Americans, 1847-1974* edited by James V. Hatch with Black playwright Ted Shine serving as a consultant.

The immediacy of the workshop is what made it possible for me to write as much as I did and as quickly as I did. As soon as a script was drafted, we would get on the stage and walk through it, reading it aloud. All of our workshops were open, so oftentimes there was an audience checking out how we developed the work. Although I continue to write plays, I am not even one third as productive as I was during the FST/BLKARTSOUTH years.

The success of the poetry performances and the drama inadvertently led to neglecting the publishing outside of *Nkombo*. For us, the written word was of secondary importance, and we never really concentrated on developing it the way we did with performance. After all, we were performing before hundreds of people monthly. We did not publish monthly, and when we did publish it seldom reached as many people as our performances did. Of course, we were making the mistake of focusing only on the present and not thinking about the future, not thinking about documenting what we were doing as a priority.

Additionally, when we did publish, we added a twist to our literary magazine that intentionally obscured the individual personalities of the writers in favor of presenting the flavor of the group. Except for the very first issue, we did not use authors' names on the poems included in *Nkombo* except in the table of contents. Flipping through the book, there was only the poems, the text itself to refer to, rather than a name above or beneath the text.

We viewed *Nkombo* as the textual voice of our collective. In my introduction "Food For Thought," I wrote:

> Blk writers' words are of only 3 forms
> 1. protest
> 2. revolutionary
> 3. blklife
>
> ...
>
> -protest writing is basically explaining to somebody how human you are, enough said
>
> - revolutionary writing is up against the wall
>
> -blklife writing is what we are

> most of what follows is directly out of our workshops where we write with only the preconceived notion of being honest to our senses, there is no pretension to it being high art

One of my poems in that first publication, "BLKARTS is the magic of ju-ju," delineated the direction our words would take:

> blkarts poets are crazy weird dudes
> whose vocabulary is in the streets&in the gutters& off the walls
> & round de corner & down the halls & whose ideas is like the same
> ones that hang on the edges of buildings where ever gathering throngs
> of blkfolk have spoken about their lives, churches, barstools & jail
> cells, jail cells, empty parking lots&the balconies of old tired cineramas

In performance, we not only read our own poems; we also developed a collective style and recited each other's poetry. Before long we had moved to the idea of developing poetry shows with musical accompaniment but only as much music as we could make ourselves. I of course played percussion but also some recorder, penny whistle and bamboo flute, plus thumb piano and occasionally balaphone.

Intuitively we had moved to the jazz band as a metaphor and model of our poetry work. The poetry shows were flexible in that they could be altered at a moment's notice. Additionally, we could reduce or increase the number of poems and the number of poets without violating the overall structure. As far as we were concerned, just as most people didn't know the names of all the members in a big band, they didn't need to know our names individually. The band was more important than the soloist; in fact, it was the band that provided the platform for the soloists to blow and develop—even the most novice poet could be accommodated and given room to recite at least one poem.

Here is one of the most frequently performed pieces that was orchestrated for the whole group. Even though I wrote the poem, I was not "the featured voice." Different people had different parts in solo or duo, while all of us acted as chorus and musicians. I remember one particular performance we did at the University of New Orleans. There was a jazz band on before us, and some of the musicians hung around for our set. The drummer and vibraphone player joined us once we got started on "Black Bones," which was how we referred to the poem whose formal title was "Names, Places, Us." This poem was published in the first issue of *Nkombo.*

NAMES, PLACES, US

Who did they kill?
What were the names of those Blacks they killed then?
No One knows no one knows
no names no places just us to witness
they are dead, killed only because their skins were Black,
we are here only because their skins were black
Who did they kill? What, where, who? Who did they kill, murder?
What?
They killed you! Who? Who dead drift now who they killed
Are you hip to the middle passage? how many of our people rest
    now at sea
their bones & flesh chewed & eaten by fish, abandoned to die in a
    turbulent sea
whipped by the frenzied hands of white masters into their places
What were the names of those Blacks they killed then
Who did they kill? What are you?
WHAT ARE YOU BLACK PEOPLE!!!!???? WHERE ARE
    YOU!!!!????
I often go down to the sea & stand looking out across
wondering
How many of my people rest now out there their bones eaten by
    fish
thrown there, in those waters, from slave ships years ago
abandoned to die in a turbulent sea whipped by the hands of white
    masters
who were they? What were the names of those Blacks they killed
    then
No one knows, no one knows, they are dead, killed only because
    their skins were Black
One day bones will wash from the sea and rest gleaming in the sun
    on eastern seaboard shores
let them then try to lie to you, let them try explaining where those
    bones come from

those bones, bones of our ancestors, dead, killed, murdered
nameless Black people, countless Black people we don't even know now
Black bones form the sea, Black bones
Bones Black bones washed upon the shore, washed upon the sand
Black bones resting in the sand from the sea, no home, no name, just bones
Legs & arms, large, small bones, Black bones Black bones thrown up from the sea
Black bones from the sea, Black bones
And when I die throw me too into that sea facing toward Black Africa
Let fish eat my hair, and my eyes, and my Black flesh
Let me go home again and if not home at least to the bottom
where I know others rest
Let me join others like me dead at the bottom
BLACK FOREVER MORE!!!!!!

Late in 1969 we published five small books of poetry: *The Reluctant Rebel* by Renaldo Fernandez, *Dark Waters* by Quo Vadis Gex, *Visions From The Ghetto* by Raymond Washington, *I Want Me A Home* by Nayo Watkins, and my debut book, *The Blues Merchant*.

I did not have any one particular style of writing. Some of the pieces were blues poems; some were wild, quasi-surrealistic screamers; some were long narratives; and some were straight out promo for whatever belief system I had at the time. In reviewing the work, I was immediately struck by a poem called "The Blues (in two parts)." Periodically I would return to this same device, writing a poem specifically about the blues that used blues images and structure.

The two long narrative poems are written under the influence of Leroi Jones of the *Dead Lecturer* period, but even so they are still very much me. They are also prophetic, as they are poems about being married and caring for a baby, written at a time when neither were yet a reality for me. There are a few conceits built into the narrative, the main one of which is that I refer to my "wife" by the initial "V," which was actually my first initial at the time. The "wife" in this poem is a composite of various women I had been close to at that time. These long narratives are precursors of my "sun songs," except that the "sun songs" in general are purposefully much more didactic.

The Blues (in two parts)

I

Our best singers
can't really sing
you take like otis redding
that nigger never could sing
in fact I believe he only knew
maybe two notes at the most
& a couple of
phrases/no melody
strictly atonal stuff
i mean like what does
yes are am mean
or even na-na-na
what's da matter baby
mr. redding you is singing
like you is in a hurry or
something, maybe you
got to go to the bathroom
& now you take that
lil ugly no singing nigger
James brown
now he can dance his
ass off, ain't no
doubt bout that
but he can't sing
not a lick &
talkin bout a
lickin stick
somebody need to
beat him all upside
his haid w/h his own
damn lickin stick

& that band
he got, they don't know
nothin but one song
that's how come
they got to have
two drummers
them two dudes is suppose
to be among the best
we got/black
people we gon have to do better
or shut our mouth
cause I mean
what is mother popcorn and
for sho dum-dum de-de de-dum-dum
ain't no song

II

The blues is not song
it is singing
no voice
is needed
only the knowledge
the blues is not
not notes
it is feeling
it is not death
it is being
it is not submission
it is existing
you take the ing
it is the ing of th-ings
whether it be
laugh-ing or dy-ing
swing-ing or hang-ing

from a tree
sometimes it be
hurting so bad
when you is singing
or feeling the blues
till you just have to
drop the g trying
to e-eeee-eeee-asssssse
on in

For my wife when I do that thing

1.
my blk girl
got out into the clearing somehow
looked out past the ocean's horizon into the sky
& it took her about
ten minutes to discover
it was blues/she returns
skipping/dancing
smiling in my stupid face
my face is ragged/toothy
sort of smile w/h big lips
through my beard
women are lovely & is
why they bear children in
stead of we men

2.
    is it still June
V. baby/pass me a color
you saw today & save
my tenderness w/h your lovely
brown fingers on my face
/she showed me a sea-shell
that was red/black inside & green
pretty -i would have passed
it by/in fact I wouldn't
even have been wading out into
the blue green water lapping
up over the seawall like she
was holding her dress folded above her knees
smiling back at me
& dodging small fishes

3.
she came home yesterday from work
tired & sleepy just before I did
like about fifteen minutes
& dinner was still on the table
"...take me to the lake
tomorrow, huh, please..."
falling about my shoulders w/h her long arms
& a kiss on the ear
she fell into my lap & told me
about the devils she worked w/h
got up ironed, washed/i dried
the pieces of plastic that replace
china in our lives—the
apartment is so small on sunny days
you seem to always be running
into blocks of heat/at evening times
i believe they call it dusk
the sun sits on the funeral parlor's roof in back of us
on rainy days it can be nice to
lay around/she is quiet like
morns when we call each other in
sick for work & loll about in
each other's arms & discuss
plans for getting up to eat
orange juice & cheese

4.
we got up early sunday
& got into the volkswagen
which had sat cooling all night
& like the lake is only 5
miles from us

5.
on the highway going further out
leaving behind the seawall & concrete beaches
i stilled the wheel w/h my elbows
trying to light a cigar
which she eventually lit for me
nearly choking twice on her laughter
on the beach's empty stretch
we had no food & sat down in the sand
& planned for a family of three

6.
my baby's eyes are big & brown
big & brown & shiny
that look at me wide open
when I am sweet to her
like bringing home a bag of
big purple plums from on my way from work
or rub her back at night
before she sleeps or be
alone w/h her
or/
    i kiss her
lips once, twice & again & again
thanking her for keeping my life
soft in her heart

7.
we love each other
& that is good
i look at her sometimes I
tell her never let her bush
grow longer/i go to work
& come home
not yet brave enough to

risk a child
    weak, weak,
weak

8.
running the risk of injury
i sat up alnight
yesterday thinking of two suitable
names, one for a girl & the other
a boy/she made me laugh, she says
"what if we have twins"
let them be, let them be
my wife & I are both 23 year old
blk folk

For my child when I do that thing

1.
my little girl's name is winnie
we call her winnie la roo
who jump happy like a kangaroo
    i use to read the papers
    regularly/the price of peaches
    has gone up steadily
    what do you want me to do/
    be
    i scowl at my wife
    alnight sometimes combing her hair
    in the mirror small tufts
    coming out in the big wide tooth ivory
    of her african comb
    turn to the wall stroking my beard
the car ran out of gas
i sat there & hit the steering wheel a few licks
"that won't do any good..."
it's bad enough she makes sense
talking softly to me w/h winnie wrapped
in a blanket in her arms
    i rolled the window down &
    hollered out it & then turned around
    & looked at her & she had her hand
    on my arm
    i called my scream back
    the car seemed too small opening the door
    letting my sandal drag against the concrete
    right on the white line/i had to push it to the side
    out of the way of bus traffic

2.
V. must of been pregnant about twenty months
trying to play like her big belly wasn't hampering her
i'd catch her sometimes smiling to herself holding her stomach
    with her hands
once in bed I laid my head on her & heard winnie moving
    around
when it came time to go I had to call a cab cause she was too
    big to get in the volkswagen
it was kind of dopey living w/h a pregnant woman
i use to could cook, winnie & V. came home to our first steak
    dinner at home
V. breast-fed winnie & I stood around looking helpless

3.
i came home friday winnie was sitting on the floor
on a bunch of newspaper mushy spinach
all over her
V. sitting on the floor supposedly feeding winnie her dinner,
    mine was on the table
they had smothered liver & carrots I went down the street to a
    local bar & had a quart of beer
when I got back V. was giving winnie a bath
"if you want to eat now I'll fix your dinner"

4.
went to my mother's house
& sat w/h an orange pop resting on
my knee covered w/h a white, blue bordered paper napkin
my wife sits looking at stupid drug store pictures
on the chartreuse walls: "i like that one"
the technique is french impressionism
but it looks like it was done w/h a raggedy handkerchief
momma pulled me to the side to ask whose idea it was to
    cut winnie's hair short like it is
"Mine!"/
        i ain't got to come here to fight
        about the way my daughter's hair is on her head

5.
went out of
town last week
for a conference
forgot to bring even a postcard back
when I got back V. was at work
so I went round to momma's & picked up winnie
& came back & had to change her diaper
& tried to feed her but she wouldn't eat
i sat in the doorway w/h winnie in my arms
looking out across the open court filthy w/h trash
& made up poems about little blk children playing stick
    ball & tag in an apartment house courtyard
the mailman came w/h bills & advertisements
winnie'll be sixteen months next week
sixteen months shaking my head

In December of 1969, I wrote in the introduction to the volume 2, number 4 issue of *Nkombo*:

> September found us performing for some of the students of Southern University in Baton Rouge, La. There, as in most other places, we were performing before people who were experiencing a blk poetry show for the first time in their lives. Many times our frankness and willingness to discuss on stage many things that some Negro's dread to even think about seemingly shocked them. Often they reacted hesitantly as we performed; wanting to laugh at times but stifling it, wanting to scream but clamping their jaws shut. However, after the show invariably they came forward to tell us that they enjoyed our work. And it was most often at the colleges where we found the more inhibited audiences. During our community performances the audiences never left any doubt as to how they felt about the shows.
>
> Every performance led to a greater confidence and also greater insight. Soon we were doing what we called "sets," i.e. poetry shows which were thematically organized, choreographed, and highly musical. We even developed a few plays which consisted of both poetry and dialogue. Within a two year period we were inspiring artistic developments all over the south, most notably in Houston, Texas and Miami, Florida.

Another factor affecting our development as both writers and performers was that Tom Dent was introducing us to cultural workers everywhere we went. Some of these people, like Worth Long, were former SNCC workers. Others were just people who loved the Black arts. Most important of all, some of the people were cultural workers right at home in New Orleans whom most of us simply didn't know, didn't know about and didn't initially understand how important they were. These included people like the poet Octave Lilly and above all the musician Danny Barker.

Danny Barker "above all" because he was a genuine African American griot. Not only was he a musician and composer, storyteller and entertainer, bandleader (he was almost single-handedly responsible for the reemergence of the brass bands among young Blacks in New Orleans), but Danny Barker was also a writer. He wrote short stories, character sketches, autobiography and history. Had not Tom understood the importance of hooking us up with people like Danny, I'm certain that our work would not have been as grounded in the community nor as lasting as much of it is.

Almost all of our attention was given to performing for our community and publishing our own work, which we sold at our readings. We simply were not into sending our work around for others to publish. BLKARTSOUTH was a tremendous development vehicle, but it also paradoxically led us away from interacting with the rest of the country outside of the South for the most part.

The best example of this is our inclusion in *New Black Voices*, an anthology that is still used in college courses edited by Abraham Chapman, who understood what we were trying to do as a collective. The poets included were Issac J. Black, Renaldo Fernandez, Kush (Tom Dent), Nayo (Barbara Malcolm, who continues to write under the name Nayo Barbara Watkins), John O'Neal, Raymond Washington and myself.

Here is one of the selections included in that anthology. It is one of my humorous poems that proved to be very popular.

[untitled]

whi/te boys gone
to the moon
plantin flags & stuff
why you boys goin
to the moon
dont yall think
yall done fucked up enuf
without messing
with somebody else's world

in the beginning
it was africa
you just wanted to see
you said
& once having seen
commenced to fucking up

open up them china gates

& let's hunt tigers in india

you whi/te boys sho nuff likes
what ever anybody else has
all ways got to be
digging in somebody's bag
always got to be plantin flags & stuff

whi/te boys done gone
to the moon
just like they come here
talking bout it's a
great adventure & we is
the first ones here
& plantin flags

whi/te boys gone to the moon
whi/te boys done gone to the moon
sho hope them lil brothers up there
dont show um how
to plant corn

In addition to the poetry, Chapman chose to include "BLKARTSOUTH/ get on up!", an essay/manifesto I wrote. The opening half of that piece is a complete summary of our intentions:

> BLKARTSOUTH started as a community writing and acting workshop under the direction of Tom Dent and Robert "Big Daddy" Costley. The Free Southern Theater had been disbanded for the year, and they were the only two left in New O. (our name for New Orleans, Louisiana) to continue on the work of the theater. By that certain inventive process that Black people are famous for possessing the community workshop grew into BLKARTSOUTH without the aid of funds, star attractions, immense programming or anything else that is usually thought of as a prerequisite to developing a theater group. We started in the summer of '68, and by October of the same year we made a vow that we would publish and perform our original material exclusively. Within a year we were performing poetry shows and one-act plays throughout the South; plays and poetry we had written, arranged, directed and produced. In December of '68 {--note: this is a mistake, it was actually 1969} we celebrated *NKOMBO*'s anniversary with a one-hundred page offset edition that included drawings, poetry, prose, fiction and drama. From the very beginning we were attempting to actualize our purpose, which was to develop and perform new/original literary and theatrical material for Black people.
>
> We go deeper now with our purposes. We say that our art is aimed toward building the nation. A nation for Black people. We say that not only do we have to be new/original but that we have to be of some use/have some meaning to Black people in the struggle for liberation. And we mean it. Since we do not operate in a vacuum, our motion has created friction and heat. In fact, we've burned up some people. But we keep on keepin on just like Shine.

BLKARTSOUTH is a whole lot of us striving toward the nation.

What we do, however, ain't mind lunges at paper targets. Our work is instead real spear movements we learned by putting our work out there. Just like the old/our folks used to wash clothes and then hang um out in the sun to dry. Hang um out where every/anybody could see how clean (or unclean) they were. The writing you see ain't academic (or un- or anti-academic either) but is some real stuff that's been hanging out in the sun. We are the results of doing/being our poems and stuff. The writing you see is not all the writing we are because you ain't seen nothing until you've heard us. That's important. That aura of hearing, feeling, seeing, experiencing this kind of writing. Our conclusions are drawn from our experiences and then maybe put down in books. Be aware of that. Be aware that the organization you are reading about is a living, performing group that produces its own material, and that the production/performance of this material is an intentional fusing of technique, content, style and ideology that necessarily gives a total shape to the whole of our work that cannot be realized or appreciated just by reading our writing in books. This does not mean that there is little attention paid to "literary" values per se; rather it means that as far as we are concerned, just being "literary" is not and has never been sufficient.

We feel that what we're doing is a relatively new thing in our environment. Our molds aren't quite set yet. Like jazz, what we're doing is constantly moving; the changing same. Right now all we're trying to do is get our work out there and be honest about the things we put out. Maybe two or three years from now we'll be able to set down some standards to judge our work by (real standards and not personal considerations, likes and dislikes, theorizing from "one-eyed" critics). Like what standard was Louis

Armstrong blowing by, other than what he felt? We can tell now, but who could have told then? Maybe not even Satchmo himself. The whole problem centers around the fact that critics invariably want to judge Black artists at their first note. They are afraid to allow the BLKARTS to grow. It took Black music less than seventy years to go from Buddy Bolden to Coltrane and beyond. So just as jazz grew, Black writing is going to grow, grow straight from the gutters, from the streets, the people. Grow from our people, which is where Louis Armstrong came from with his trumpet playing, his eye-opening innovations. He got it all from a culture that accepted, emphasized and respected an African inspired, African American heritage of music making. We as writers have a similar heritage we must tap, a spoken, verbal art that runs deep and long all the way back to the homeland. Slave narratives, field hollers, shouts, hard luck stories, animal tales, everything. A real heritage we have been taught to ignore and belittle, a heritage we must get next to or be like a tree without roots. We must grow to know this heritage and do as it advises us: Sing about what we are in a good strong voice and not get caught up in trying to imitate others or denying the worth of what we are. Sing our own songs.

We at *NKOMBO* say that our goal is not to put out a magazine full of "little poetic masterpieces" but rather to publish a journal that will serve as an adequate medium of expression for Black artists of the South. We feel that Black writers are ignored (and as a result stunted in their growth) by the traditional publishers both Black, such as they be, and white. Many critics insist that there is very little "quality" Black writing available as an explanation for this exclusion. But the truth is that there is too little Black writing available period, "quality" or not. And furthermore there will never be a large body of so-called "quality" Black writing until there is an even larger grouping of Black writing published irregardless of "quality," a larger grouping that is written to reach and take in Black people rather than to live up to some vague flat-cultured concept of "quality." That sounds cold, defensive and anti-good literature, but it's true. It's an unbelievable trip to think that the absence of quality is the cause for the exclusion of Black writers when there is so much garbage being dumped on the heads of our people by white publishers. Check it out for yourself. Go to any local bookstand or drugstore and pick out what you consider to be quality writing. After you've done that, look at all the junk that's left. Quality??? Not hardly. And that's what we're out to change. Black writers are not published simply because the publishing industry is for the most part white and doesn't want to or doesn't know how to publish Black writing (that's not meant as a criticism but rather as a realistic assessment of fact and intentions; like we ain't out to publish white writers either). Our policy is that those Black writers who live in our area and participate in our workshops will be published, period! We are intent on making sure that any writer who is interested in writing will be able to get at least one of his pieces published in *NKOMBO*. The future will decide what is of "quality." Let that be taken in, let it remain; throw the rest away.

We've been around for three years now darting in and out of the consciousness of Black people in the South and elsewhere. We feel like we ain't even off the ground yet, still just pecking away at this eggshell environment. But as soon as we break out of this straight jacket society/mind condition . . . we movin on up! We want to move, got to get away. Our art is functional art that's going to help all us Black people find ways to fly. We trying to get Black people together so that we can all consciously make that great migration east. To quote brother Kush (tom dent), "anyway, our poetry, the beautiful thing about it has to do with making connections with, talking to, grooving

> with blk people, not with 'poetry' or 'great writing' or being a literary giant or an ideological father or any such shit as that. Just making connections, giving blk people something they can value and use. This is what we mean by functional writing." If somebody can learn something from it or it draws Black people closer together, then our writing has done its do.

The other major exception to the trend of a low national profile was our inclusion in *Negro Digest/Black World* edited by Hoyt Fuller. We were always included in the annual *Black Theatre* roundups even though, as Tom pointed out to me, we were often the ones who had to write about the theater scene in the South because no one came down from New York or Chicago to write about what was going on. But even so, this was more attention than we got from any other source outside the South.

As one of the most developed writers in the workshop, I did publish regularly but not as a poet. Except for one of my plays, *The Destruction Of The American Stage*, almost all of the pieces I published were either directly related to our theater work, or were political essays or cultural critiques. In 1971 I won *Black World*'s first Richard Wright Award for excellence in criticism.

Besides Tom Dent, of all the other people in the workshop, only Lloyd Medley had a poem published in *Black World*. While I was working on this manuscript, I ran into Lloyd in the post office. He reminded me that his poem had won a first-place award for a first poem published by a new writer. Before I could tell him the thrust of my reference, he went on to echo my sentiments: what we were doing was as strong as, if not stronger than, the work of many of the other writers of our time, but we weren't in New York or on the West Coast.

Although we both recognized that had we published more, we would have received far more recognition, achieving "fame" was really not our aim. This may seem unbelievable, but the fact is we were happy doing what we were doing. We were traveling throughout the South. We were performing. We were publishing our own work. We were influencing others. And we were young. What more was there?

Although we certainly wanted our work to be entertaining, we avoided like the plague simply being "entertainment." Always, for us, the work needed to be relevant. Relevant to the people in our community: to the kids and to the elders, to the working class and to the daughters and sons of the working class attending college, many of them the first in their families to do so. Invariably, we challenged our audiences and critiqued "Negro" ways of thinking/acting. Our humor and sarcasm was withering. But there was also a great deal of warmth in what we did and an overwhelming love for our people, which was reflected in our love for each other. Again, because we came from New Orleans, we were a bit distrustful of a unity based on uniformity. We preferred the concept of a gumbo composed of diverse elements.

Our orientation was to include everybody in the pot and not to exclude someone just because they were of a different persuasion. This was not always easy, but it served us well. For example, I remember when some of us became Muslims. Even though most of us changed our names (in 1970 at one of the first Kwanzaa celebrations in New Orleans, I had taken the Swahili name Kalamu ya Salaam, which means "pen of peace"), not all of us converted to any particular religion or any particular political organization.

Philosophically our workshop covered a wide range of opinions and beliefs, and we tried our best to express the widest degree of tolerance. Can you imagine that within one poetry group we had practicing Catholics and practicing Black Muslims? Moreover, because we were from New Orleans, our skin hues, social/religious backgrounds and individual expressions covered a very broad spectrum. One of our members had naturally blonde hair and blue eyes. Undoubtedly our collective's spectrum of hues contributed to our concept of blackness, which stressed consciousness and culture much more than phenotype.

My point here, and our point then, was to contextualize our work in Black community and culture in its many facets. Whereas many artists were extremely uncomfortable with this sort of contextualization at that time, the process spurred our development. I say "our" because not only I but a number of other writers and theater people (including Tom Dent, Nayo Watkins, Chakula cha Jua, Johnetta Barras, and Quo Vadis Gex Breaux) have testified to the value of what we achieved, attempted and learned from our experiences in FST.

Two other important points. One, we never believed that everybody had to do the kind of theater we did. Ours was a voluntary commitment, and as poet Mari Evans pointed out in an important article first published in *Black World*, those who volunteered were not being forced to parrot any particular line. They chose to believe and create out of their beliefs and experiences.

The second important point is that our collectivist view did not ipso facto lead to a lessening of artistic development in terms of technique. Certainly no one would argue that Lorraine Hansberry wrote shrill propaganda or that she did not write well. She wrote exceedingly well; nevertheless, she also believed in the social function of art: "I persist in the simple view that all art is ultimately social: that which agitates and that which prepares the mind for slumber. The writer is deceived who thinks that he has some other choice. The question is not whether one will make a social statement in one's work—but only what the statement will say, for if it says anything at all, it will be social."

While working at FST/BLKARTSOUTH, I had decided I would be a writer, a professional writer. Later I expanded that vocation to include being a producer, mainly because a lot of the artwork I desired to experience and to share with others didn't exist, and it needed a midwife if it were to be born. Here again, the example of Langston Hughes impelled me forward without hesitation: my obligation as an artist was to create—and whatever necessary ingredients for creation were missing, well I would just have to marshal them by whatever means necessary.

In the final analysis, in this period I saw myself as an artist, a writer, a dramatist, a performer, but also as an active participant in the liberation struggle. I saw no separation between the two; indeed, my whole professional life has been aimed at merging the two so that they are not only inseparable but also each developed to its most effective pitch.

five. a decade of development

> *My goal is to uplift people, as much as I can. To inspire them to realize more and more of their capacities for living meaningful lives.*
>
> *—John William Coltrane*

By the time *Hofu ni Kwenu (my fear is for you)*, my second poetry book, appeared in 1973, some of the BLKARTSOUTH crew had started Ahidiana, an activist-oriented collective. Around the same time, FST closed down for a lack of funds. Due to an argument between John O'Neal, one of the FST founders, and some of us from the workshop, BLKARTSOUTH split off on its own. This was the same period in which Ahidiana was founded.

Ahidiana ran an alternative school for preschool through third grade-aged children—and we always made sure that kids from working class backgrounds were the majority of students. We were not interested in operating a little "private academy" populated mainly by the children of Black professionals.

We also had a food co-op to buy fresh fruit and vegetables. We had a small garden. We operated a bookstore and owned and operated a press. We brought speakers and activists (such as Amiri Baraka, John Henrik Clarke, Mari Evans, Yosef Ben-Jochannan, Maulana Ron Karenga, Haki R. Madhubuti, Sonia Sanchez, Owusu Sadaukai, and Sweet Honey In The Rock) to the New Orleans community. And finally, we organized around community issues and around Kwanzaa activities.

Our organizing work included demonstrations against apartheid and police brutality, as well as challenges to the mainstream media based on FCC-mandated community access issues (which the Republicans dismantled as soon as they got in control at the federal level). Our organizing also included annual Black Women's Conferences, which attracted attendees from around the country.

Our experiences in FST/BLKARTSOUTH helped us understand how to organize and how to dramatize issues, raising the quality of our political presentations to a very high level. Concomitantly, the political issues sharpened my artistic work, making it both more explicit and more specific. Even though we had moved past simplistic sloganeering, I still had a lot to learn about writing poetry. Ahidiana was my graduate program.

Here are two poems that exemplify the merging of the artistic and the political. The first is a poem in support of the political prisoner Dessie Woods, who was imprisoned for killing a White man who attempted to rape her. She never denied the shooting. This was a favorite performance piece. It is an ironic commentary written in the feminine voice, a technique I developed not as a gimmick but rather as a way of making a statement about the particular issue at hand, as well as a broader statement about how I felt revolutionary male writers should be supporting the feminist anti-sexist struggle. Most often when we performed this type of work, either Shawishi St. Julien or my wife, Tayari kwa Salaam (with whom I also co-wrote two children's books in the Ahidiana years) voiced the poem.

The second poem is a defense of Ntozake Shange that was published in an issue of Al Young and Ishmael Reed's *Quilt* magazine. This poem was written and published during the backlash against Ntozake Shange that many males were whipping up over *For Colored Girls*. This was the kind of piece that put me at odds with some of my fellow male writers. That was OK with me; in fact, I enjoyed the confrontation.

We in Ahidiana believed that confrontation of contradictions among our people was healthy as long as the contradictions were debated and hopefully resolved without resorting to violence among ourselves. I was aware, however, that in certain circles this piece amounted to "fighting words."

HIWAY BLUES

(for Dessie Woods)

ain't it enough
he think he own
these hot blacktop hiways,
them east eight acres,
that red Chevy pick up
with the dumb bumper stickers
and big wide heavy rubber tires,
two sho nuff ugly brown bloodhounds
and a big tan&white german shepherd
who evil and got yellow teeth?

Ain't it enough
he got a couple a kids to beat on,
a wife who was a high school cheerleader,
a brother who is a doctor,
a cousin with a hardware store,
a divorced sister with dyed hair,
a collection of Hustler magazines
dating back to the beginning,
partial sight in his left eye,
gray hairs growing out his ear,
a sun scorched leathery neck that's cracking,
a rolling limp in his bow legged walk,
and a couple of cases of beer in the closet?

Ain't it enough
he got all that
without having to mess
with me?
Yeah, I shot the
motherfucker!

NTOZAKE SHANGE

(to those who wish
she would shut up)

I.
if yr life had
happened to a man, the
whole world would know abt it,
but you a big-legged woman
breaking the monopoly of male writers
talking bold about what has kept
you from walking off the ledge of life
and what drove you out the window
in the first place, about to
silently hit the sky falling
like a dropped drum stick
during the middle of the big number

II.
talk abt yrself
yr blkwomanself/neo-african
in the midst of a land caught up in
worshipping twentieth-century minstrels

talk about womanness and exaltations
and never uttering the lie about being
sorry not to be born a boy, talk
like you think, like you feel,
like you move through decaying urban america
pass fashions, kitchen recipes, modern romances
and mythical holy vaginal orgasms
talk like our moses spake
in the middle of headin' north night
pressing a slack-jawed man who

couldn't keep his pants dry:
"once we get started, ain't no turning
back!"

talk like that lil sister, can't
remember her name, who shot hot
breath all up in a white boy's face
and double-dared him to fuck with her
in the hallway, in class, after school, on
the bus or any other goddamn time, back in
1958, in one of their schools when,
at the time, you did good just
to stay proudly black and defiantly sane

talk like you an oracle
bearing witness to changing times
or the sphinx sitting on the secret
in the desert, not only was you blk
but, yes, possibly you were woman
when napoleon saw that he barked
the order for his battery
of cannons to commence
and left part of your nose,
and a piece of lip
pulverized and floating
a dusty cloud toward the nile

talk that talk
when the truth is revealed to the
light, the shysters will all scream
'taint fair, they'll cry
foul, say yo strikes smokin
clean down the middle are misses,
say you high, or low, or wide,
or you got spit on the ball,

you see you just ain't allowed
on the mound and there you
are talking like you ain't
never heard of being
quiet and pretty in the bleachers

talk Shange, talk
like a lioness putting
her jaw around a jackass' throat

III.
to some men
the sound of blkwomansong
is noise

but no matter,
many of us are dancing anyway
and in time most all of us will be waving
red bandannas and shouting: "amen,
amen, sister, amen"

well.
well.

Ahidiana was a product of its time. Today there is no similar Pan-African movement, nor was there any similar Black liberation struggle in the nineties. Yes, there is the Afrocentric movement, and while I hear and understand a lot of the theory, the practice is not community rooted or community dependent. Further, the majority of the Afrocentrism leadership is based on college campuses and predominantly mainstream campuses at that. Nor is this movement linked to international struggles, which was another driving force encouraging our efforts in the early seventies.

Hofu was the first book produced by Ahidiana, and it reflected our activist orientation. We described it as "A collection of essays and poetry written by Kalamu ya Salaam that explains and defines the natural functions of men and women and the relationship between men and women." From *Hofu* on, every poetry book I wrote during the Ahidiana years came out of specific social contexts and was meant to influence our community at large and to directly affect those of us engaged in the Black liberation struggle.

Those who have never volunteered to be a cultural guerrilla at war with the dominant and dominating culture probably cannot understand both the exhilaration and the freedom involved in creating socially committed literature.

The exhilaration is perhaps more obvious than the freedom. It is both humbling and uplifting to present your poetry and witness people react in honest and deep-felt ways. To see people laugh and sometimes even cry; to have people come up to you, their eyes shining about how your work helped them make it through the semester, through a marital dispute, while in jail, while in the army, etc.; to hear people chant your poems back to you, hear them clap and pat their feet as the audience participates; to hear them shout out to you, *teach*, *right on*. To be there at the creation of a new consciousness, that is exhilarating—an exhilaration unknown to the literary poet whose work is appreciated in solitude. For here we have the circle completed; the feedback loop is immediate. Here we have the actualization of one of the cardinal tenets of the Black aesthetic: immediate "call and response."

The calabash of community is reconstructed; the circle is unbroken. At the deepest level one must ask what is art without an audience? Furthermore, if audience is necessary for art to exist, then should not the involvement of the audience be as timely as possible? The audience responding not only exhilarated us; it pushed us to produce more and better art, art that was cleaner, leaner and more pure in its connection with the audience.

No matter what "thought" we had, the test was to find a way to communicate it. How to convey the concept of dialectics in a poetry reading at a community center, on a playground, to preschoolers, at the college campus. Our audiences were wherever our people were, and our challenge was to reach all of them. Of course, this required crafting and composing different poems for different segments of the community and also required us to expand the general conception of poetry, but as we became better and better at it, we perceived each challenge not as a problem but rather as an opportunity. This was an exhilarating time.

The freedom of it is less obvious but no less real. Essentially it boils down to the fact that we had no masters. We had broken off the plantation of literary poetry and had no maps, no set destination, no preordained models to which we had to adhere.

We had to be truly creative. We had to improvise. There were no sacred cows. We could quote anyone we wanted to or quote no one. We could use techniques from traditional poetry or invent techniques based on music. We had the seventies atmosphere of revolutionary freedom. Our freedom was precisely that we could use any and everything we wanted to in whatever way we wanted to.

Some of us wrote in rhyme; others of us didn't. Some of us had a college education and had been exposed to all kinds of literature; others of us were people with a deficient public school education (when integration came, the quality of education that we had received at schools like Phillis Wheatley and Rivers Frederick suffered a serious decline). Some of us were writing in dialect;

others of us weren't. The principles of the Black aesthetic guided us: it's not what you do but the way that you do it.

Moreover, because our people are human beings who represent the broadest spectrum of emotions and intellectual proclivities of any community in the United States, there was always an audience for almost any style of poetry we wanted to write. Plus, we had numerous poetic examples to draw on within our own culture: from the jazzy surrealism of Bob Kaufman (who was from New Orleans) to the formalism of Robert Hayden, from the hip street talk of Don L. Lee/Haki R. Madhubuti and Sonia Sanchez to the literary arcaneness of Melvin B. Tolson and the classical rigor of Gwendolyn Brooks, it was all there for us.

Sonia would be killing with her signifying pieces one minute and kissing us with the awe-inspiring quiet of a haiku the next. Baraka could make us scream out loud or send us scurrying to a dictionary to figure out what he was talking about. And that was just on the creation side.

On the audience side, the people who came out to hear us were so hip. Some of them knew more poetry than we did. They would give us tips. Tell us about poets, some of them locals whom we had never heard of and whom we needed to know. Whatever idea we dropped, usually there was somebody in the audience who would pick up on it and afterwards want to rap about "that thing you said, well, you know I was thinking..."

In our audiences you might find a person who had ardently studied Shakespeare sitting next to a barroom bard for whom toasting, signifying and reciting his own version of "Shine" was the highest form of poetry. Our task was to reach both of them, to feel free to draw on both of their experiences, and to use all of that and more of that in everything we did.

For us being Black was a blessing. As Americans we could learn from and, if we chose (which few in our collective did), we could even emulate the mainstream literary world—and at the same time, as African Americans we could draw on a rich culture of orature that the literary mainstream knew little if anything about. Moreover, we had our music (the only major American contribution to world culture) and our people's musical usage of English to draw on. We had so much, so much.

With so much happening daily around you, there was no excuse not to write. In this context, work just poured out of me. I would write about everything: hanging my foot out the window after making love, a demonstration against police brutality, hair styles, dance styles, Pan-Afrikanism, sexism. The window was throwed up high, and fortunately by the seventies I had been writing for over a decade so I had a degree of facility that comes from practice, practice and more practice—plus, I had an audience.

I was writing for the members of Ahidiana: I wrote wedding poems, praise poems, poems and songs for our kids who were now appearing with regularity. I was writing for the community: all kinds of demonstrations were happening, and a rally wasn't a rally until at least one poet was called upon to give some "poetic inspiration." All kinds of Black journals were popping up, and there was always a need for a cogent and timely or topical poem.

I was also writing for myself. If I couldn't express myself in poetry, it just meant that whatever I was trying to express was unclear in my own mind or else what I was thinking was out of phase with what I was feeling. In that sense my poetry was very, very private in its origins and orientation even as it was public in its expression. That was the dialectic that made the most sense to me. As I worked out ideas, theories and understandings of whatever I was experiencing or grappling with, I would know I had reached a degree of understanding when I could put it in a poem and communicate it to others.

Eventually I called these poems "sun songs" because they were partly sermons delivered in the style of Baptist preachers and partly because they invariably relied on musical motifs, musical metaphors and musical organizational methodologies and techniques. I would beat on podiums, stomp on floors. Sing. Shout. Jump up and down. Dance. After all, I was a poet.

Hofu will always be fondly remembered as my first poetry book that was more than just poetry: the cover was a symbolic piece created specifically for the book. Inside we had symbols as well as text. We also mixed essays with poetry, and the poems included both tender and tough pieces. The book was printed in green ink on ivory stock. It set the aesthetic tone for all the other Ahidiana publications that followed.

You could see growth happening in this book, but you could also see glaring blemishes, particularly a vehement strain of homophobia that Ahidiana would directly tackle within the next four or five years. I know some people would say that homophobia was just part of the times, but there is no need to hide from the truth. On that account, we were backward. Other poems and essays that tackled homophobia head on would follow over the next few years, and thusly demonstrate through both criticism and self-criticism that regardless of where we started from, we kept on developing.

In 1973 we were what I would now call classic Black nationalists. Even though we thought we were being progressive, our position on the women's question was also suspect. That too would change over the next couple of years. *Hofu* would have been stronger artistically if I had been more progressive politically. The feeling was there; the ideas were lagging behind. *Hofu* was then both experimental and limited, but it was an attempt to move past status quo examples of what a poetry book should be like.

Here are two selections that demonstrate where we were at in 1973. The first piece, "Lament" is written in the feminine voice and actually had been written somewhere between 1967 and 1968; it was published in the first issue of *Nkombo* and because of its subject matter, I chose to include it in *Hofu*. Audiences used to get really, really quiet when we did this one.

The second, "Inspiration," is an example of some of the most progressive thoughts cohabiting with some of the most regressive. I used both the word and the image "faggot" in a negative sense. In later years, I would continue using the poem but substituted the word “freak.” Also, in performance this poem was built on a chain gang chant, “Be My Woman,” which Nina Simone also used a variation of in her song “See Line Woman.” The chant metamorphosed into a Curtis Mayfield-like ballad, “Love A Good Woman,” and ended on a Pharoah Sanders tip. Of course, the music is not on the page, but this is an example of how I wrote poems that were designed to be sung, as well as spoken, lyrics.

LAMENT
for black men everywhere

when
  will our men be men
    not of fear and trembling
    feeding dark soil with their own
  dark blood or
    crying yes sirs and halting steps
  of broken airs about
  themselves
but men:
  simply able to love their lives
  as men are said to do?
God can you possibly
  replenish that lost seed
  who were once lovely African chieftains,
    princes and such, loving
    their queens
  Can pride be restored
  or must they suffer forever
  attempting a shield of their
  impotence from our knowing eyes.

INSPIRATION
THE FLOWER IN THE HOUSE,
THE AIR WE BLACK MEN BREATHE

love a good woman
love a good woman
for all the time there is
for all the life there is
for all the best we are
love a good woman
love a woman
love love a good woman

in sunshine, in rain, place
yr house in order, in
balanced on the tear drop of her happiness
on the hair back from her geled* head
on the soft steps she makes
moving toward you being the flower in the house
yr oxygen, yr gettin up fuel
yr no nonsense and strength to do what you got to do
the love of a good woman
loving you love a good woman
yr choice, companion and soul mate,
yr maker really, if you be man
then woman is yr maker, yr woman is yr maker
yr black woman is yr creator, woman
is what you should love yr good woman
is what you need yr good woman to love, to live
yr pleasant voice in the evening and smiles in yr morning
yr soft fingers touch on yr chest calling you king
calling you man, calling you god
you god the giver come on now love yr good woman
she creator the maker, love yr good woman
no man makes himself

woman makes man and love
love a good woman

sister i am incomplete
without you, i am vessel full
of holes, i am spirit begging
substance, i am shadow with
our form, i am baby wait
ing to be born, i am that faggot
walking down the street
not knowing what to do with myself
like singers without song
i need yr tender touch

*head wrapped respectfully Afrikan styled

In January of 1973 Ahidiana published my third book of poetry *Pamoja Tutashinda (Together We Will Win)*. In advertisements for *Pamoja* we described it as "A collection of political poems with an introductory essay by Kalamu ya Salaam that is a beginning projection of the ideology of Pan-Afrikan Nationalism." *Pamoja* had a cover by Fred O'Neal, who had done the cover for *Hofu*, and was printed in black ink on a light tan paper.

This was the most didactic of all the books, strictly an organizing and conscious-raising tool. One of the poems, "give a speech/ talkin abt 'da problem' " is five typeset pages long in nine-point type. The five-part poem was read at many a rally.

Part one poetically asks the question:

give a speech to reach
the masses, to reach this, to reach us
who are tired of words?
give a speech

Part two responds to the question with cynicism, which is itself responded to:

somebodies, some bodies are sayin
that's the problem nah
niggers talk too much
but is it? is that
really the problem now
    is talk why our life expectancy is so short
    is talk why we eat so badly
    is talk why we work a week for one day's
        wages
    is talk why everybody laughs at us on
        television
    is talk why we spend so much time in jail
    is talk why we have no money, no power,
        no land

is talk why all our schools are dumb, our
 teachers dumber
is talk why nobody likes us
nobody likes the Negro
is talk the cause of that
are we here because of talk
think about that,
did talk rape your grandmomma, red?
did talk make you eat pork, abdul?
did talk cut off the gas&lights last night,
 rhetta?
did talk do this or was it organized people
taking advantage of our ignorance

Part three rhetorically asks the question: "do we want out of this" and, assuming the answer is yes, goes on to suggest:

then organize
organize to control
control the space we occupy,
control all that space as best we can
the first space being of course, the body,
 the flesh and
muscle, brain and mind body, control that
 from hair tip
to toenail, discipline it i.e. self-control it
exercise power over it i.e. self-determine it,
 self-defend it, self-respect it

Part four speaks directly to how to organize:

start with the easy, give a dime a day
start with the easy, run one block a day
start with the easy, read for five minutes
 a day

start with the easy, eat one fruit a day
start with the easy, volunteer fifteen
  minutes a day
start with the easy and organize to do the
  undifficult
don't worry about the heavy problems
all the heavy problems ain't goin nowhere
just develop self step by step and one by one
we'll get to everything in due time

Of course, many, many people reject this as poetry, especially people who are not overwhelmed with social problems and actively seeking a solution. Similarly, people who are relatively comfortable with the status quo reject this as poetry. But what difference does the theme or content of a poem make in terms of whether we are dealing with poetry? It is not the content that makes a poem a poem, but rather the style and presentation.

In 1973 I made another major move. For two years I had worked as the first director of the Lower Ninth Ward Neighborhood Health Center. I had also been a founding member of *The Black Collegian Magazine* in 1970. Both the health center and the magazine were growing. I was offered the assistant directorship of the whole neighborhood health care system with the promise of becoming the director within the next year and a salary of over $25,000 per annum with benefits. I enjoyed the work of directing an outpatient health care facility located in the neighborhood where I had grown up—but I couldn't do both. So, I quit.

By then, I knew what I wanted to do more than anything was write. I never will forget: right after signing the contract papers to work at *The Black Collegian*, I went to the city welfare department, applied for food stamps and, based on the small salary I was drawing at *The Collegian*, I was eligible. I never regretted the move.

The Collegian offered me the opportunity to develop my writing and editing skills. Additionally, I had the opportunity to offer activists in the movement a platform to speak to Black college students across the country. I interviewed a wide variety of activists, artists, and politicians. I was even able to help Hoyt Fuller when John Johnson closed down *Black World* and fired Hoyt. One of the early issues of Hoyt's new publication, *First World*, was published in *The Black Collegian* as a special insert. My stay as an employee of *The Black Collegian* paralleled my membership in Ahidiana, which had been officially founded in the summer of 1973.

The following year I was selected as a delegate to the 6th Pan-African Congress held over the summer in Dar Es Salaam, Tanzania. That trip marked the beginning of an ongoing pattern of traveling around the world as either an activist, a writer of socially committed literature or a journalist. Before long I went to the People's Republic of China, Cuba, Surinam, and numerous destinations in the Caribbean. At the same time that I was developing as a poet and performer, I was also traveling around the world meeting, being inspired by and learning from activists and artists. My outlook was expanding quickly as a result.

By late 1975 with two strong years of organizing and operating under our belt, Ahidiana began to get serious about radicalizing our position on the women's question. The next book came out early in 1976. *Ibura (Swahili for "something special, miraculous or wonderful" and also our third child's middle name)* was dedicated to my mother, who had passed on 5 October 1975. The whole book was about women. In addition to the poems, *Ibura* contained two short stories, one of which was later published in Sonia Sanchez's *We Be Word Sorcerers*.

There are two poems in this collection that have particular meaning for me: "Top 40" and "Ibura/Come Get To This."

"Top 40" was written for Maxine Maye, a good friend who lives in Washington, DC, and who was a stalwart in the independent Black school movement. "Top 40" demonstrates one of the techniques I frequently employed: using the experiences of close friends as both a sign of how deeply I appreciated them as individuals and also to create poems that addressed lessons for our community at large. Almost all of my work, regardless of theme or content, draws on real lives (myself, my friends, our community, the world) for details. Sometimes it's as minute as using a color as an image because a friend might wear that color often.

In any case, "Top 40" was a very popular poem at readings. It opens with a cataloging of pain:

babies, no babies
children, single & multiple
employment, exploitation
scar tissue and wounds
anger, hurt, disappointments
...
weary, certainly, of the centuries
of the necessary but nonetheless crippling
and often unacknowledged work of forced
  soloing,
sometimes seemingly single handedly
having to handle the process
of propagating and preserving
our subjugated race, our
wounded pride and indeed, our
historically tested humanness
you are, i'm sure, tired
of being cursed and accused
for the umpteenth million time
of being damn aggressive
when not aggressive but human,
female and Black in a time
callous & cruelly hard on such a combination
and too, terribly tired of taking shit
and knowingly pretending it's sugar
...
don't let her be misunderstood

This was a three-part poem based on a classic country blues form of AAB, i.e., make a statement, repeat the statement perhaps slightly paraphrased or altered, and then conclude with a statement that commented on the opening two statements.

In part two we amplified the opening:

babies, no babies
house, apartment, bus
stop, street corner, car
man, husband, lover
(scarcely ever three in one)
and still seldom someone there
who actually understands
or even consciously tries to

the continuous struggle,
what to do,
supporting the dead weight
of unconscious brothers,
those bad black bodies pressing down
upon your breasts, but betrayals
notwithstanding, true to who you
actually are, you move on
giving sex, or giving money, or giving love,
or attention and indeed, giving your whole
aching life, giving that
taking that, not taking that
but moving on, liking life
hating it, wishing
you were dead, or joy
so in love, yet always
always moving on
Black woman, black woman
i hear you
i see you

Then the third part sharply contrasted with, but did not contradict, the two-part litany of realities faced by women. What I was trying to empathize with was the real situation faced by women and especially by single women, such as my friend Maxine. Musically, this particular poem has an analog in Bill Wither's exquisite song, "But She's Lonely," even though I actually refer to an Al Green song.

...at a window, looking out
and looking in and just sitting sometimes,
stopped for a short moment
for a fast minute
just momentarily resting, catching breath
just, just basically reflecting
on the conditions of our collective existence,
cognizant and courageously critical of
the serious realities of our struggle,
unsurrendering, your voice is absolutely
bittersweet but strikingly strong as you
sing silently softly along
with the top 40 song drifting
pervasively around the solitary sunlit room,
from the radio...
"...i'm so tired of being alone,
i'm so tired..."

Where "TOP 40" had been addressed to the sisters, "IBURA" is a sun song addressed to both sisters and brothers. There is no way that I can help you hear it except to ask you to read it aloud and think of a preacher at the pulpit. There are numerous musical references in the poem, some of them obvious ("Billie singing"), some of them obscure ("keep our eyes on the prize of life, hold on, hold on" referring to a freedom song from my civil rights days). The dedication is to Yvonne Mason, whom I had first met during our civil rights days when she and her sister Yvette joined our picket line. Later, in the mid-seventies, I would meet Yvonne again when she was working as a typesetter for Edwards Printing Company, the company that first printed *Nkombo*.

Ibura was printed in black ink on aqua blue paper stock. It had artwork by Arthello Beck, a Dallas-based artist whose work I came into contact with through *The Black Collegian*.

IBURA/COME GET TO THIS

(for Yvonne A. Mason & many, many more)

Many of our brothers are actually afraid
somehow of you, feel weak in your presence,
sort of emasculated by your strength or so they say.
Can not stand your corrective gaze, find it near impossible
to move when you are in charge, so they question your
femininity.
But is it you who should be questioned or we? Are we really
men, if we can not deal righteously with our women,
our beautiful black women, who have remained toughly
together throughout this terrible tumultuous travel
cross water into new world named america? Our women who
have never stopped getting up, giving birth and supportive
succulent sweet satisfying love, never once stopped walking
home, alone, night after night, carrying big brown bags
full of clothes and used food to feed us, stolen from day work,
or sad hours spent silently suffering degrading labor
in offices and backrooms for chump change under the
lecherous eyes and hands of capitalist crackers.

Our women, our women, who, even on pain sometimes of death,
have never denied loving us. Remember Billie singing
"if it's one thing that I've got, it's my man and I
love him so!" Our black women who will wear their hair
anyway we want it, if only we knew what we really wanted,
our women, Tubman steady, Sojourner strong, Parks steadfast
Big Mama wise, young sister sensitive and song singing soulful.
Our women from town and country, life to death, something sure
to count on, consistent like sun rises, life bringing
life spring rain falling, our women, beauty catching in the throat
and the most nourishing love that a man can have and hold. Do
we

understand that they, our women, are a guide given to us
to keep our eyes on the prize of life, hold on, hold on.

What we need now is a saner society, we need to create a place
where life can be lived to the max, enjoyed, improved and made
ultimately much, much better than when we arrived, we need to free
our women from all our own twisted anti-female chauvinistic
thoughts and actions, sad actions, many of which were frosted on
us by dog lovers, johns and assorted other individuals who
come crawling forth from caves with weird ideas about women,
sometimes refer to themselves as "he-men" as opposed to their
women whom they sometimes call she-men which explains partly
how they really view life. What we need to do is encourage
our sisters growth, encourage our women to get together and
speak out, to rush forward and take the lead on social and political
issues, to form associations that will organize around their concerns,
we need to be there supporting them in each and every way like we
like to envision them supporting us. What we expect of them is the same
as they need to have come from us. Like we need wives, they need
husbands, like we need love, rest and relaxation, they need the same,
need what we need, need us like we need them.

After *Ibura* came *Revolutionary Love*. Even though *Iron Flowers*, a short book of poetry inspired by a trip to Haiti, is the tightest thematically, I still think *Revolutionary Love* is the strongest of all my poetry books from this era. At 114 pages plus fold-out illustrations, *Revolutionary Love* certainly was the largest book of poetry I had ever published—it contains more poems than all of the previous books added together.

It is also the most overtly political even as it has some of the most "personal" poems I wrote during those years. It contains the clearest articulation of what we came to mean by "art for life," our alternative to "art for art's sake," which we rejected. Certainly here I articulated the Ahidiana philosophy more cogently and with greater artistic skill than in any other collection of poetry. In *Revolutionary Love* the actualization most closely matches the intent, and the articulation is artistic to the max.

While none of the sun poems in *Revolutionary Love* are as strong as "speech" in *Pamoja*, overall there is a greater diversity, and technically I achieved some alliterations and metaphorical reaches that still make me smile. Two of my favorite poems are from *Revolutionary Love*—actually there are about fifteen or so poems in this collection that are my personal favorites of all of my work from this period—but I won't bore you with my personal preferences.

"Personal preferences" is an inside joke, referring to the distinction we made in Ahidiana between what we called a "political point" as opposed to a point of "personal preference." The collective arrived at and agreed upon political points, but each individual had a right to hold points of personal preference. Most of us, of course, would frequently exercise our rights of personal preference to explain why we liked or disliked a certain thing, idea, action, person. This allowed us a way to express disagreement without getting disagreeable.

At Ahidiana we actively studied political theory, Amílcar Cabral being our most respected theorist, and were very much into criticism and self-criticism. We even developed position papers that delineated a methodology for both giving and taking criticism. While all of this probably seems strange and a bit far out to people who are used to functioning as individuals, in the context of a collective, there was always a need to monitor the motion of the group lest we end up in a state of cultish self-delusion. The balance for us was our ironclad rule that we made decisions by consensus: if and only if everyone agreed would we establish a rule, take a political position, or commit ourselves to an action.

Other organizations and individuals repeatedly criticized us for our rule by consensus, but it served us well and kept the more articulate from browbeating the less articulate into accepting something that not everyone was prepared to accept. Just the knowledge that each individual had veto power forced all of us to be sharper in presenting our ideas. We knew we had to convince each member.

Again, this probably seems to be a very restrictive situation for an artist to be in, but exactly the opposite was the case. The majority of my work from that period was sharpened by group criticism, and I was emboldened by the knowledge that these ideas were not simply artistic idiosyncrasies but valuable insights shared by a close community of committed individuals.

Of all the poetry books, I think *Revolutionary Love* best fulfills the promise of *The Blues Merchant*. There is a definite diversity of styles in the same way as that first book of poetry had except that I was by then a much better poet, as is exemplified by these two poems.

The first poem is part of our ongoing struggle to move beyond race/racism as the sole definition of our condition. The second is an example of self-criticism.

all that's black ain't brother

1.
white people
come in all colors

their systems sink
past skin
anchoring into bone, mind
flesh, heart and soul

it is geno-suicide
to minstrel aliens
but some of us do die
strangled by our own
hands

2.
some of us
selfishly think that
self starts
and stops
with i

dream not of peace
but money, don't
dance, hate
our energy
and lust for
an equal opportunity
to turn the screws

see that
black boy over there,

he's white.

Diapers and Dishes

i can thrust
my hand straight
into the toilet bowl, expertly
swirling a soiled diaper around
shaking loose all the stool
as I submerge the cotton cloth
agitating with a firm
back and forth action

i used to recoil
from the touch and texture
of warm masticated corn
kernel hulls and other leavings
smellingly ejaculated
from our babies' behinds
but now it is no bother

i used to be upset
coming home late at night
shake my head and suck
my teeth at the sight
of dirty dishes in the sink
now I willingly wash them

these tasks are so simple
since my thought
has been reformed

Tayari can read now at night
since we share housework
and mutually develop
now, after much self struggle, i
too can change
diapers and wash dishes

i laugh at my old self
sulking about bowel movement
and toilet water on my hands
or dishes that need only
a little time and hardly any
trouble to be made clean

i laugh at my old self
if feels good to improve

In a feature length profile of me published in a local weekly, writer James Borders judged:

> "More congenial now to dialectics, ya Salaam's work in *Revolutionary Love* reverberates with a new fullness that is more deeply personal and more deeply social than any of his past attempts. It is all statement, and it has found its most effective distance. Published by Ahidiana and printed on the group's own press, the poems and essays that comprise the text are gorgeously embellished by the drawings of Douglas Redd and the photographs of Kwadwo Oluwale Akpan. If the words don't grab you, the visuals will."

Borders was impressed by the total package, which is exactly what we intended. Early on in FST/BLKARTSOUTH, we were using drawings and photographs in our publications as well as text. This was because a number of the members were visual artists as well as writers and because as we continued, both Tom and I believed it was important to include the visual artists in the presentation of our work. Eventually, we would also begin inviting blues and jazz musicians to perform with us.

These developments were not accidental. We aspired to a holistic concept of the arts, even before we had the theories to articulate and rationalize why we did. We felt it and went with our feelings. Later, we would be able to define what our feelings were.

By the Ahidiana period we were going all the way. Ahidiana had a performing ensemble, composed of musicians and singers as well as poets, called the "Essence of Life." The name was taken from a song by Gary Bartz and Andy Bey whose chorus was "we must get closer to the essence of life." Essence of Life produced a weekly radio program for six months or so, in addition to owning and operating our own press—not just a publishing company but an actual printing machine, which was run by Kuumba Kazi, a member of Ahidiana who had previous experience operating a printing press. We were serious about actualizing the principles of self-determination and self-reliance.

All of this affected my writing. How could it not? What may sound like fantasies and exaggeration cold on the page actually had a social basis in that we were an active organization whose total goal was to turn words and ideals into revolutionary deeds. Everything we did was designed to raise the liberation struggle to a higher level. We were much more than just talk; we were action—and that action inspired me to write like I had never written before.

The final book of poetry in the Ahidiana period was *Iron Flowers*. A trip to Haiti in August 1979 affected me so strongly that I started writing the book during the last couple of days in Haiti and finished everything within a matter of days upon returning. For this book the cover and borders were done by Douglas Redd, who by then was the main artist I worked with. But the book also included photographs I had taken in Haiti. Next to *Revolutionary Love*, I like this one the best from cover to cover.

Again, there are two poems that stand out. One is the last selection in the book, titled "Tomorrows' Toussaints." The other is "Beyond The Boundaries," the poem I most often read from this book. *Iron Flowers* was printed in black and red ink on the cover with black only on the inside, on a translucent, semi-parchment, eggshell-white paper.

Tomorrows' Toussaints

this is Haiti, a state
slaves snatched from surprised masters,
its high lands, home of this
world's sole successful
slave revolt, Haiti, where
freedom has flowered and flown
fascinating like long-necked
flamingoes gracefully feeding
on snails in small pinkish
sunset-colored sequestered ponds

despite the meanness
and meagerness of life
eked out of eroding soil
and from exploited urban toil, there
is still so much beauty here in this
land where the sea sings roaring a shore
and fecund fertile hills lull and roll
quasi human in form

there is beauty here
in the unyielding way
our people,
colored charcoal, and
banana beige, and
shifting subtle shades
of ripe mango, or strongly
brown-black, sweet
as the suck from
sun-scorched staffs
of sugar cane,
have decided
we shall survive
we will live on

a peasant pauses
clear black eyes
searching far out over the horizon
the hoe motionless, suspended
in the midst
of all this shit and suffering
forced to bend low
still we stop and stand
and dream and believe

we shall be released
we shall be released
for what slaves
have done
slaves can do

and that begets
the beauty

slaves can do

Beyond The Boundaries (meditating on the meaning of life)

I.
who am i
who visits
who stares at sights
who strains to catch the
drift of conversations
who bathes
who dresses
who eats
sometimes two or
more times a day?

what does my black skin
mean to similarly skinned people
when there is money
in my pockets
and no pockets
on their pants

or
when I glide pass
at a hundred kilometers
an hour as they
trudge step by step
cross rolling mountain side?

these are tense questions
testing my thought

II.
who asks for their lot
who chooses parents, or
selects birthing spot

i have I.D., U.S. certified,
but what is my identity
Haiti haunts me
there are eyes I saw
in those hills
in the silence of those
noisy nights, Haiti

i turn over
back to the wall
even in the dark
i keep seeing me
beyond myself
climbing to the side
of some overfull tap-tap*
singing out in comfortable tongue

"keep going,
keep going, don't stop
i'm alright!" Haiti,
are we,
are we alright?

congealed into too many urban areas
our people idly littering stolen streets, oh
these spaces are so bitter
Africa has had
to walk so many rough waters
we need rest
we need rest but must
press on, "keep going,
keep going,"
never mind that the
particulars of our nativity
are luck and circumstance

what we do
with our after birth
is the singular
importance

III.
who knows what Toussaint
lurks in the heart of Haiti
how can we new slaves
of an old world order
not be Haitian
not have fight
and freedom flowing
in our veins
flashing, flaming like
gold shooting through
sturdy human hills

never mind the language,
a barrier, breakthrough
the dress code
a barrier, breakthrough
the lay of the land
a barrier, breakthrough
breakthrough, yes
individualities do differ
but essences, our
essences rise and converge

IV.
go beyond the boundaries,
where we're coming from
matters
matters so much more
than where we've been
where we were born

if we fail to recognize
that there is no one
human who is totally foreign
then we ourselves will
fail to become anyone
oh Haiti, Haiti
Haiti, heart of hurt
Haiti, heart of hope
you hit so hard
at the meanings of life

the call of
conch shells
caper so softly
cross our verdant
land, cross valley
cross water, Haiti
everywhere
we hear your history
somewhere slightly west
of here, in Jamaica, we say
i and i

i and i
meaning I am
i and I am
you and you are i
and you are you and
it is getting late

and I fall asleep
awakened
by this important
Haitian hiatus

and become a
different person
more conscious
of all I am

At the time I had no idea how true a statement I had made regarding becoming "a different person." Ahidiana had survived the split in the Black nationalist movement, which might crudely be characterized as the cultural and/or revolutionary nationalists versus the neo-Marxists. By the early eighties we began to sense a development that we had not foreseen, one which, in retrospect, had been accurately forecasted by Fanon in *The Wretched of the Earth*. Essentially, the Black Liberation struggle fractured, and much of the energy that had previously gone into organizing oppositional activities and alternative institution building was now going into participation in electoral politics and reform-oriented activities.

The first successes at getting Black politicians elected inevitably led to more and more people jumping on the electoral platform. The Congress of African People gave way to the National Black Political Assembly. It was as if the whole Black nation had been persuaded that the best course of action was working for reform from within the system rather than continuing to build alternative institutions outside of it. Yes, we really were becoming different and most of our nationalist oriented organizations, Ahidiana included, did not survive past the mid-eighties.

In June 1980 we produced my last Ahidiana book, *Our Women Keep Our Skies From Falling*. *Skies* was my most radical and effective work. The title was a paraphrase of the Chinese proverb that "women hold up half the sky." The essays, written "In support of the struggle to smash sexism and develop women," reflected our most thoroughgoing critique of sexism. By its publication we were also presenting lesbians at our annual Black Women's Conferences.

This book was popular in women's groups across the country. Both complete essays and excerpts were reprinted in newsletters and anthologies. Some of the essays were published in major Black journals of the period, including *The Black Scholar* and *Black Books Bulletin*. But even more popular than the essays were two of the poems: "Pa Ferdinand" and "...And Raise Beauty To Another Level Of Sweetness." Each poem has a story.

Skies was dedicated to my father. When people would ask how did I come to such a point of view as expressed in my writings, I would invariably point to my father. From the civil rights days on, he actively supported me and my brothers. When I joined FST he told me with pride how he had been involved in drama at one time. When we went into revolutionary struggle at SUNO, including arming ourselves, he supported me.

But more than all of that, he always evidenced a respect and love for Black women that never failed to inspire me. He would bust our behinds at a moment's notice, but he never struck my mother; in fact, he seldom even raised his voice, even though he was quite sarcastic in talking about some of her teacher friends, whom he kindly described as "phony."

On the back of *Skies* there is a portrait of him and me standing next to the pecan tree in our backyard, which he planted when we first moved there in the mid-fifties. He was so proud of this book, and I was proud of him. "Pa Ferdinand," a tribute to my father, was included by Ruby Dee as part of the text of an article she published in *Ebony* magazine.

"Raise Beauty" is altogether different. It was actually written as an advertisement for a special Black woman's issue of *The Black Collegian*. The brochure advertising that issue was sent out to recruiters across the country. I didn't care whether they understood the poem or not; I wanted to make a statement of support for Black women. Over the years, church groups and community organizations would reprint the poem as well.

The community's acceptance and use of both "Pa Ferdinand" and "Raise Beauty" embody the most profound example of what we considered to be the usefulness of revolutionary Black art, whether a personal statement such as "Pa Ferdinand" or a straight out political statement such as "Raise Beauty."

PA FERDINAND (on this man's foundation i build my political support of feminism)

my father
is a solid stepper
amid a generation
of soft shoers
& scuffling shufflers

was young with
WW II, did not die
nor get discouraged
but rather fought
on both fronts
and unflinchingly brought
the fight back
home, after
korea

a country boy
who walked miles
for school & job
he married the minister's
daughter (who was
a school teacher)
but never went
out to lunch for
class or church,
could sing but usually
kept his baritone
at home
i remember him home
making us work
rising with the sun

and planting food
in the city

i remember him home
waxing floors
on his knees
and requiring his sons
to follow his lead learning
to cook and clean

but mostly
i remember him man
teaching me
consistency: the
importance of principle,
the necessity of
struggle and the
immense beauty
of interrelating
with a good woman

what more could
a son receive
from a father
than the realness
of life lived
like a conscious
African(american)
man!
sho-nuff simply doing
his duty, in his own
context, in his own
space and time.

...AND RAISE BEAUTY TO ANOTHER LEVEL OF SWEETNESS

You are a fresh flower
bursting boldly
into a hard world
with a softness
strong as steel

Reaching for sunlight
you raise yourself
up from down under
out of the degrading dirt
society has so routinely
dumped on women,
you have transformed
manure, muck and mire
into fertilizer

Springing self assertedly
past winter weather
you bring a sweet fragrant
incense and inspiration
into musty places
stale with the stuffiness
of misogynic sexist
status quos

You blossom, you bloom,
you expand and grow,
raising beauty
to a bedazzling higher
and healthier level of
light, life and love

Grow on Black rose
Black woman grow on!

Ahidiana continued to publish pamphlets and journals until its closure. After *Skies*, much of my time was taken up with political organizing. When Black power zigged toward electoral politics, I zagged. Shortly after Ernest Morial was elected the first Black mayor of New Orleans in 1978, I was one of the leaders of a takeover of the mayor's office around the issue of police brutality. That was the culmination of one phase and the beginning of another.

By 1983 I had left *The Black Collegian*. And that was just the beginning. Piece by piece, the foundation and inspiration for my artistic work crumbled, and I was forced to reexamine everything: everything I believed, everything I had achieved, and every dream I had ever conceived; it was all a touch and go, day-to-day struggle to survive. Although I would write a great deal throughout this period of questioning, it would be a long time before I would publish another book of poetry.

Six. The Reconstruction Of A Poet

> *"There is never any end. There are always new sounds to imagine, new feelings to get at. And always there is the need to keep purifying these feelings and sounds so that we can really see what we've discovered in its pure state. So that we can see more and more clearly what we are. In that way, we can give to those who listen the essence, the best of what we are. But to do that at each stage, we have to keep on cleaning the mirror."*
>
> *—John William Coltrane*

In 1985 I wrote a haiku that perfectly expresses the turbulence and searching that engulfed my life at that time.

haiku #7

summer rain showers
fall; in renegade silence
i strip search my soul

I had left Ahidiana, left the *Collegian* and was shortly to leave the Jazz & Heritage Foundation, after beginning work there in 1983. Most emotionally wounding to me, I had also left my marriage.

The breakup of my marriage deeply hurt me precisely because my "ideology" couldn't save it nor could my deep "respect" for women and commitment to anti-sexist struggle. The breakup forced me to come to grips with understanding why women occupy such an important role in my life and why I often write in the feminine voice.

The answer begins back at the beginning. For example, the blues woman I helped register to vote does not exist. She is not an individual but a composite, not simply of the women I met doing voter registration work, but also a composite of my perceptions of those women. But why is she so important?

She is important because Theresa Copelin, my grandmother on my mother's side, was important to me. Theresa Copelin reared me up until the time I went to grammar school, and Theresa Copelin also released me from the tyranny of organized religion. She was the minister's wife, essentially the queen mother of the church. The most socially revered female I personally knew. My grandmother whipped my butt when I did wrong. But when I left the church, rather than whipping me with words or making me feel bad, she gave me a lesson in compassion.

I had been groomed to be a preacher in the tradition of my grandfathers. While still in grammar school I was reading verse and making statements from the pulpit. I quit going to church in high school. At the time, it did not seem like a big deal to me, but for my mother and my grandparents it was the end of a dream.

In the customary metaphorical directness common to pre-sixties southerners, my grandmother acknowledged my decision not to take up the call of preaching. One Sunday after church, before I quit attending altogether, we were all climbing into my grandfather's car, and my grandmother told a joke. She said there had been this young man who had been coming to church regularly. The young man declared he wanted to preach because God had called him to do so. Shortly afterwards he announced that he was going into the seminary to become a preacher.

Well, the church didn't hear from him for a while, and then one day he came back. Everybody was glad to see him. They asked had he become ordained yet. He said no. They asked what happened, hadn't God called him? One of the deacons said, when God calls, it's best that you answer. I did answer, the young man replied. Well, then what happened? Well, said the young man, when I got there, God told me never mind.

All through my life there were strong women, caring for and teaching me every step of the way even when they didn't necessarily agree with me. That blues woman was also my mother, who was the only teacher in her school to go out on strike, and then after the strike was over, she returned without bitterness to work with and, yes, befriend her fellow teachers. My mother was that blues woman when she gave me this advice, which sustained me in the awful decade of the eighties: "Do whatever you think is right, but always be prepared—no matter what anybody else may say or do—always be prepared to go it alone."

That woman was certainly also Mrs. Nelson, my English teacher, and Mrs. Green, my civics teacher who actually taught Black history.

So then this is why women speak in my work. They not only created a major part of me; they also created the emotional space for me to be myself. How could their voices not be sounded by me?

Why then has my later work championed gay rights and spoken forcefully against homophobia and heterosexism? Did I have experiences with men that I've never revealed in print? Of course. But these experiences were not sexual in nature. They were instead bonds of comradeship and friendship.

Remember when I spoke of Hoyt Fuller. I remember writing a long essay on homosexuality in the Black Arts Movement of the seventies. I sent the essay to Hoyt Fuller at *Black World*. He commented that it was an interesting analysis from a heterosexual position. But he did not publish it.

When Hoyt died, I spoke at his funeral and wrote a praise poem for him. My biggest disappointment was that I had not created space enough for us to safely discuss Black gay realities and experiences. I vowed to work to create such a space for serious discussion and respect of the "other" in our community, howsoever the "other" is defined.

Again, my life is also inseparable from my New Orleans acculturation, where I would see gay men who affirmed their identity simply by refusing to disguise themselves as straight men. They moved about, especially in the entertainment world, as though there was nothing in the least bit unusual about themselves, and that was liberating for both them and ultimately for us who witnessed and came into contact with them. For example, there was Bobby Marchan, a singer who had worked with Huey Smith and the Clowns. Bobby was also a well-known emcee of rhythm and blues shows. He would do a standup routine that flaunted his homosexuality, and he especially enjoyed taking on macho hecklers.

Then the contact became more than an observed phenomenon; it became an integral part of our liberation struggle. While at SUNO, one of the people who made sure that our newsletter, *The Black Liberation Express*, came out on time without fail was gay. I could never deny that brother's commitment nor his competence. Later, after some of the BLKARTSOUTH members joined the Black Muslims, there was a gossip campaign about one of our major members. Did I know he was a "faggot"? Did they know that that didn't matter?

I realized through those and numerous other experiences that confronting homophobia required courage on the part of homosexuals and bisexuals who also wanted to participate in the liberation struggle and the Black Arts Movement or who wanted simply to be able to walk hand in hand down the street without being stoned.

One day, coming out of the New Orleans Jazz & Heritage Foundation's office, there was a gay man at the bus stop and a woman who looked at him hard, seemingly with daggers in her eyes. He literally crossed the street.

I turned to one of my coworkers and said, "People laugh at men like that, but they have no idea of what his struggles are and how much courage it takes for him to openly be the way he is."

The verse play *Malcolm, My Son* was born that day, one example of an expression not only of solidarity with the "other" but also an appeal to the rest of us.

Some of what has made me what I am I will be able to remember only with great difficulty, the difficulty of keeping the mirror clean. If I am a true poet, eventually it will all be revealed—or my efforts will at least bare as much of my history as I can (under) stand to uncover.

Social conventions are clothes on our psyche. The poet must be a worshiper of nudity and, therefore, be precisely in opposition to the merchandisers and social bureaucrats (e.g., government officials, business administrators, religious leaders) of the status quo, whose essential tasks are to sell uniforms and to enforce dress codes. To be a poet is to be at odds with the present if only because every dominant status quo has something to hide, something that needs to be revealed.

In this same period, I wrote a poem whose whole focus is on the question of the role for poetry. The poem is structured into call and response. In introducing the poem, I would reference "*Viva la revolucion!*" and ask the audience to respond with a strong "*Viva*" every time I said the word "poetry." I would tell them, however, only shout "*viva*" if they agreed with what I said.

The poem was actually inspired by an English/Spanish bilingual reading I did with Cuban poet Pedro Sarduy. He had written "The Poet," a poem about being a poet, which he recited in Spanish. I recited the English translations after each stanza. I was impressed by what he had written and decided to do a similar kind of poem, hence the "*viva*" response, which by the way does not appear in the text of the poem.

THE CALL OF THE WILD

Poetry is not an answer
Poetry is a calling
    a vision that does not vanish
    just because nothing
    concrete comes along, or
    because the kingdom of heaven
    is under some tyrant's foot

Poetry is not a right
Poetry is a demand
    to be left alone
    or joined together or whatever
    we need to live

Poetry is not an ideology
    poets choose life
    over ideas, love people
    more than theories, and really would
    prefer a kiss to a lecture

Poetry

Poetry is not a government
Poetry is a revolution
    guerrillas -- si!
    politicians -- no!

Poetry is always hungry
    for all that is
    forbidden
    poetry never stops drinking
    not even after the last drop, if we
    run out of wine poets will
    figure a way to ferment rain

Poetry wears taboos
    like perfume with a red shirt
    and a feather in the cap,
    sandals or bare feet, and
    sleeps nude with the door unlocked

Poetry cuts up propriety into campfire logs and sits
    around proclaiming life's glories far into
    each starry night, poetry burns prudence
    like it was a stick of aromatic incense or
    the even more fragrant odor of the heretic
    aflame at the stake, eternally unwilling
    to swear allegiance
    to foul-breathed censors
    with torches in their hands

Poetry smells like a fart
    in every single court of law and smells
    like fresh mountain air
    in every dank jail cell

Poetry is unreliable
Poetry will always jump the fence
    just when you think poets are behind you
    they show up somewhere off the beaten path
    absent without leave, beckoning for you
    to take your boots off and listen to the birds
Poetry is myopic and refuses to wear glasses
    never sees no trespassing signs and always
    prefers to be up touching close to everything
    skin to skin, skin to sky, skin to light
    poetry loves skin, loathes coverings

Poetry is not mature
    it will act like a child

to the point of social embarrassment
if you try to pin poetry down
it will throw a fit
yet it can sit quietly for hours
playing with a flower

Poetry has no manners
it will undress in public everyday of the week
go shamelessly naked at high noon on holidays
and play with itself, smiling

Poetry is not just sexual
not just monosexual
nor just homosexual
nor just heterosexual
nor bisexual
or asexual
poetry is erotic and is willing
any way you want to try it

Poetry

Poetry has no god
there is no church of poetry
no ministers and certainly no priests
no catechisms nor sacred texts
and no devils either
or sin, for that matter, original
synthetic, cloned or otherwise, no sin

Poetry

In the beginning was the word
and from then until the end
let there always be

Poetry!

While I did not belong to the church, as "The Call Of The Wild," makes clear, I was a preacher. The Bible was not my text; my poems were, my sun songs especially.

I also believed in the "spirit" and in "possession," after all I had been reared Baptist. I remember once being in the choir stand when the spirit hit a young sister my age. She was thin, and my brothers and I were hefty. I never will forget being unable to hold her still when she fell thrashing to the choir floor. I looked into her eyes—she was not there; something or someone else was, and she was making some sound, or should I say some sound was coming out of her; it was not screaming; it was something else. On other occasions, I have felt myself almost crying (what do I mean almost—I cried) just listening to a choir singer.

Even though I left the church, I still wanted to be a conduit for the spirit, for that spirit. Sometimes in poetry performances, I reach it.

In *The Bluesman: The Musical Heritage of Black Men and Women in the Americas*, author and blues musician Julio Finn describes the role of the preacher in the prototypical Black church. Finn perfectly described the function I aspired to as a poet:

> ...the black preacher performs his sermons. Standing straight and stiff would never rouse his congregation; he shouts, whispers, threatens, pleads, jumps, dances, quakes, sings—in a word, he seeks to conjure his flock, to bring them to the state where they can be possessed by the Holy Ghost. 'Can you feel it?' he screams. Next instant, he is in a trance, rapt in the divine spirit, on the brink of revelation. At a flick of his hand the music mounts, the voices of the choir lift on high, and the tranquil glory of salvation descends. No black preacher will last for long if he is no good at transmitting his emotions to his assembly. It is no good feeling called to preach if you can't make your auditors feel your message. This transmission and the communal experience of God exists because they literally

> feel the power of the supernatural passing through their own minds and bodies. The 'fits' black Baptists fall into are but the 'possession' of the Vodun by the loas. Only the names of the gods have been changed, in order to protect the innocent.

When I recited my poems, I was a preacher not simply in style but also in my inclination to instruct, to delineate good from evil, to inspire to prescribed action, and in my elucidation of the finer points of my religion (my ideology).

As the eighties went on, however, I began abandoning the politically oriented sun poem in direct proportion to my own distance from the practice of (as opposed to the belief in) socialism, revolutionary nationalism. This shift was moved from a push to a shove to a fall by the general failure of the progressive movement to defeat capitalism and neocolonialism in the Third World. There was literally nowhere where we succeeded.

Of course, I still wanted to be free. But when I look at the structure of my poetry after 1983, I notice that I am less inclined toward the sermon style on political issues. Now when I take up the sun poem, I speak not as a preacher from the pulpit but rather as a blues singer on a stage articulating hurt, pain, suffering and the withstanding of the same. Now I really have the blues.

No longer is the blues simply a form that I feel is relevant; now, in the face of all the changes, all the disappointments, victories denied, now, me, my life is the blues. I am not singing from racial memory. I am not singing for effect. I am singing my own song.

There is a confessional tone, a revealing of what life has been like for this traveler—truth told, weathered by the weight of failures albeit buoyed by compassion for the world and leavened by a sincere appreciation of the ultimate great goodness of life that only realizing oneness with the world can bring.

So I still write sun songs, but now these are sagacious praise songs for my cultural traditions rather than optimistic revolutionary anthems. Whereas before I sang a song of my people and for my people as a witness, now, like the blues bards of old, I witness my own living for surely my living has become part of the history. Structurally, I am now more interested than ever in singing the blues—there is a melancholic edge in my voice—it's just that I don't have to go anywhere to find it because the blues has found me.

Question: what happens when a poet who has functioned in a collective for over fifteen years and has had all of his poetry books published by a collective suddenly finds himself alone? Answer: nothing—literally nothing.

Although I knew and was known to numerous influential people in the Black Arts Movement, I had never published a book with anyone outside of New Orleans and only rarely had published single poems. Moreover, I was completely outside of the college lecture circuit. When the movement slowed to a trickle and my own involvement also shifted, I was left on the outside. I had to reorient myself and in the process, I examined not only my own history but also the entire body of African American poetry.

From the very beginning, Black poetry has consisted of two trains running. One train accepted and emulated the Eurocentric literary traditions, and the other train rejoiced in and propagated the folk-based, orated (semi- or quasi-musical), indigenously developed African American expressions. This is not simply a question of theme or content but also a question of technique.

A poet such as Michael Harper without question writes thematically from a Black perspective, and his work is particularly expressive and suggestive of the music; however, over the years his techniques have become more Eurocentric in a literary sense. Is he, therefore, less "Black"? Of course not. He's just on the westbound train, that's all. The same is true of Jean Toomer. His book *Cane* is considered a classic of African American literature. Part of the reason that it has achieved that stature is because its technically accomplished ("brilliant" and "gifted" is how it is often described) poetry is generally rhymed and in iambic pentameter and therefore accessible to literary critics. Although it's carrying coal, the poetry of *Cane* remains a westbound train.

In the preface to the 1970 edition of *The Poetry of the Negro*, coeditor Arna Bontemps writes: "If the compilers had sought for a racial idiom in verse form among Negroes, they should have concerned themselves with the words of Negro spirituals, with folk rhymes, with blues, and other spontaneous lyrics. These song materials, no doubt, suggest a kind of poetry that is racially distinctive, that lies essentially outside the literary traditions of the language that it employs. But the present anthology consists of poems written within that tradition, by Negroes as well as others."

There we have it clearly stated: even Negroes have excluded the eastbound train when dealing with literary concerns.

Moreover, if the eastbound poets are perceived as threatening because they are on a train headed in the opposite direction, then is it not also understandable that there will be limited publication and support of their work? In February of 1994 I served on an NEA literature panel. It was expected that I would be familiar with the work of American poets and, in general, I was. One proposal we adjudicated referenced Haki R. Madhubuti. I was the only African American on the panel of eight or nine. No one else was familiar with Madhubuti's work.

Haki R. Madhubuti has over a million books in print! He is America's best-selling African American poet. I would have been considered "unqualified" to sit on an NEA poetry panel if I were unfamiliar with the work of a contemporary White poet who had sold more than a million books of poetry and was also the head of a major publishing company, but the reverse was not true.

The majority of oral-oriented, African American poetry is unknown to America's general literary world. Most Americans have never attended a Black poetry reading nor heard any of the few recordings that are available. There is a wall of ignorance. Breaching that wall has not been my main concern, however.

One of my goals has been to develop and articulate a theory of poetics from an Afrocentric point of view. I wanted the theory to be more than a simple description of a few techniques or a reductionism to "dialect" combined with overtly "Black themes and content."

For me a major part of developing theory happens through the conscious praxis of writing poems with very specific goals in mind. While I am no less interested in writing political poetry, I am much more interested in investing the politicalness of the poetry into the structure of the poems.

I think it is both fatal and facile to slip into the quagmire of using a biological definition of race (as is the case for a majority of the establishment's considerations of blackness) to define aesthetics. At Ahidiana we defined blackness as color, culture and consciousness; I took the first for granted and set about the task of defining culture and consciousness. I began "constructing" poems that detailed a particular facet of Black social existence and that painted an overt picture easily grasped but that also had an underlying political thrust. The politics of this poetry is sometimes unconsciously intuited by the audience or, at other times, subconsciously ingested.

For example, "A Moment in a Mississippi Juke Joint," was written as a direct effort to deal with those who criticize social realism as unpoetic, based on the old joke about Soviet movies of the sixties: Q: "What do you call a Soviet romantic film?" A: "A Man And His Tractor."

My effort was first to use the image of a tractor as genuine eroticism. Second, I wanted to deal with "peasants," which in my case was translated to Mississippi country folk. Third, I wanted to employ only those images that such people would know intimately. Fourth, I wanted to present these people with a positive sense of self-esteem and an aesthetic of personal beauty based on an appreciation of their own physical features.

a moment in a mississippi juke joint: wilma mae looks at john l.

his slender eyes
and taut behind, bared arms
blackberry dark with grapefruit
sized biceps, but especially
the massive slope of his head
with broad textures like the benin
bronze she didn't consciously know about
but subconsciously gravitated toward
and those teeth shiny like
lighthouses down on the gulf coast
flashing through the ink of stormy night

wilma mae looked at his feet
and the go slow grind of his hips
keeping time to the juke box
& sucked her breath in slowly, she
would have taken a seat
except she was already sitting with
her thighs pressed tightly closed

just then john l. threw his head
back and sprayed the ceiling
with the mirth of his laughter
and casually did a little dip
on the off beat of the break
in the undulating song

"god," she thought "that man
look like a tractor, & i feels like
a field what ain't never been plowed..."

By now I had also figured a way to make an oral statement and simultaneously make a textual statement: don't combine them, separate them. "A Moment..." uses a song fragment, "oh, you poor, lovesick child," as a call and response device, but that device is not written as part of the text. Instead, whenever I recite the poem, I explain the call and response to the audience. Thus, I achieve the participation of the audience as part of the orality of the performance, and at the same time, I can develop the text without worrying about how to include the oral.

Of course, this means that the poem on the page ceases to be recognized as a lyric. Were it not for the explanation, the reader would have no way of knowing that there is even a performance aspect tied to the poem. While this approach does not work in every instance, I have found it the most effective in allowing me to fully develop the oral as well as the textual potential of a poem.

Another example of this technique is the poem "Tasty Knees," which was written as a critique of the view of sex that centers the male orgasm. I chose to deflate the penile fixation by ironically elevating it and then revealing the alternative. When I recite the poem, the tempo increases, mimicking the act of making love. I get louder and louder ending on the word "ejaculation," and then I deliver the deflating line "of course, I'm exaggerating." Invariably people laugh. But the critique is actually delivered by having the poet celebrate an aspect of lovemaking that is not phallus-oriented, namely the "tasting" of knees.

Many people do not realize that much of what we have been taught as good writing is structurally based on a patriarchal perception of copulation. Is it not true that the high point of a story is called the climax and if a story goes on too long after reaching a climax it is said to have "petered out"? These are the philosophical questions with which I was consciously dealing.

Tasty Knees

in the dark of touch
my face pressed heavy
to your head i open
my eyes and see the
night hair of you dark
as the lightless black
of a warm womb's interior,
your wetness inviting touch
your earth quakes, shakes and opens
as my rod my staff
slides across your ground
though i want to scream i
resolve to remain mute
as a militant refusing to snitch
to the improper authorities, but
suddenly, a riot of joy breeches my resolve
and i disperse the moist quiet of our union
with an involuntary shout loud
as a bull elephant's triumphant ejaculation

of course i am exaggerating, but my, my, my
your knees did taste some good, yeah

In 1989 I produced and recorded *A Nation Of Poets*, featuring Amiri Baraka, Pearl Cleage, Haki R .Madhubuti, Wanda Coleman, Mari Evans, Askia Muhammad Touré, Sonia Sanchez, and myself. A CD of that event was released by the National Black Arts Festival (NBAF) in 1990. I also self-published *A Nation Of Poets*, a small book of poetry featuring all of the poems I presented.
I made no serious attempt to distribute or directly sell *A Nation Of Poets*, due in part to the fact that I absolutely abhor self-promotion. All of my adult life as a professional writer had been spent pushing the collective rather than any one individual. After twenty-five years of functioning in one way, to suddenly begin self-promotion as an individual is not only very, very difficult, it is also distasteful.

Although the seemingly simple work of pushing my book was not my speed, serving as the producer (conceiving of and coordinating all of the activities and supervising the recording) for the NBAF poetry program was both acceptable and arduous but relatively uncomplicated for me to see through to successful conclusion. Similar programs at the Schomburg Library and for the Caribbean Cultural Center in New York followed.

I also produced and recorded New World Poets for the Houston International Festival in April 1991. The New World Poets were multicultural: African Americans Jayne Cortez, Haki R. Madhubuti, Thomas Meloncon and myself; Asian American Genny Lim; Chicana Evangeline Pinon; Native American Jack D. Forbes, and Puerto Rican Tato Laviera. All of us worked out of a strong oral tradition. I coordinated and recorded a poetry night in New Orleans featuring Amiri Baraka from Newark, Jimmy Santiago Baca from New Mexico, John Sinclair from Detroit, and myself from New Orleans.

In November 1991 I produced Bright Black Words, a special two-nighter at the Contemporary Arts Center. The program featured New Orleans poets Labertha McCormick, Arthur Pfister, and Mona Lisa Saloy, along with myself and the Word Band and a workshop production of my verse play *Malcolm, My Son*.

In 1992 *Malcolm, My Son* won an award from Rites and Reason Theatre at Brown University. This two-person play deals with the definition of manhood in the context of young, gay male coming out to his mother.

Writing it in verse was not a premeditated act. I was not trying to make a sentimental statement; I wanted an overtly political statement. But I realized this was an emotionally charged issue, and as I got started, I also realized that poetry was easier to do than dialogue. For one thing, I was not trapped into using "realism" or even "chronology." Once I got started it took only four or five days to complete. Here is an excerpt in which the mother, Amina, responds to her son's questioning about the uniqueness of his condition.

MALCOLM: Were there ever any other gay men in our family?

AMINA: If you open the closet in the hall,
If you root around in the corners of the attic,
If you dig in the crevices of basements,
Go to the old picture books
And look into the eyes of our blood...
The felt hat worn across that great aunt's eye
With a man's tie dividing her breasts,
The big-eyed youth hiding on the edge of
    the picture
His hands clasped in his lap staring with terror
At something way beyond the camera...
In the tear-strewn trail
Of all those still-missing ones
Who left home and disappeared
Somewhere across the Rockies or into
The soft belly of Europe,
The cousin you never heard from again
After he reached fifteen and left the church choir

And had the beautiful voice
That broke your heart to hear him
Reluctantly sing goodbye,
Or the one you only heard from through
Occasional phone calls at odd times
During some randomly selected decade...
Like I said, this is nothing new.
We just keep pretending we've never
Dealt with all this before, pretending.
But we are now no more sick
Than we've ever been during this sojourn
In the wilderness of being forced to make do,
Striving, although often valiantly failing,
To create wholeness from the twisted scraps
Of what's left after labor rape
And racist assault on our human selves.
(Pauses.)
Do you understand?

The Word Band was a poetry performing ensemble that I directed during this same period. We had Kenyatta Simon, a percussionist, and two vocalists/reciters Maria "Gingerbread" Tanner and Anoa Natambu.

The Word Band, now in hiatus, was my most advanced articulation of poetry as music. Most of the poems were my own, although we also had "Answers In Progress" by Baraka and a Mari Evans poem in our repertoire. What was sweet about The Word Band is that I figured out a specific musical reference for each piece and then did specific arrangements. The idea was to function as a band playing specific charts but also to maintain, indeed to require, improvisation. Each arrangement had cues so that the band members would know when to make the changes. While the poems were always in the foreground, they were recited as music. I consciously set out to cover the entire sweep of Great Black Music—everything from elemental blues and a cappella gospel moans to really "out" new music a la late period John Coltrane, Archie Shepp and Pharoah Sanders.

Many people talk about jazz as a model for their poetry; most mean simply that they reference the music. Some quote the musicians; some sing the music; some list song or album titles. Some even describe musical scenes or do comparatives between a quality and a known musician ("as blue as B.B. bringing black blues by stroking the strands of Lucille's singing hair"). While I share those techniques, I also believe there is a deeper region.

Other possibilities include using actual music forms: the AAB or AA'B of classic country blues, the AABA "standard song" form and the more complex forms pioneered by Duke Ellington, which are basically structured on theme-variation (A, A', A") within a three or four part development such as A, A'/ BBC/D. This translates into an introductory statement with an embellishment, followed by a classic blues statement/statement/contrast or concluding statement, and finished off by a coda.

Theme-variation (A, A')—with the A part established by a specific word or phrase that is repeated at the beginning or the end of a line—is a very common device in Black poetry, although I'm not sure how many poets consciously work with this form as opposed to simply using it because it feels like the technique to use.

In addition to form there is also the use of words as sound and rhythm devices rather than for a specific meaning. This is particularly true of non-conventional, slang, and so-called "curse" words. In Black poetry the word "shit" is not used solely to literally refer to excrement. In fact, in the Black lexicon shit is a completely neutral word in and of itself. Its meaning (if there is a meaning) is purely contextual and sometimes, even then, it's used as a structural device to achieve rhythm, rhyme or inflectional emphasis.

Another option is the employment of "dirty" tones, which refers to playing notes off-pitch or sliding in and out of intonation. One can alter spelling to conjure both the original meaning of the word as well as a comment on that meaning. One of the more common examples is spelling America in this way: "Amerikkka." Another way to use dirty tones would be to repeat the word with variations such as "America, Amerikkka, A Merry Caw, A-Murderer."

These are just some examples of structural approaches to poetry based on music. In this regard, some of today's rappers are really inventive in their word play and reflect a blues sensibility in how they rhyme.

My effort with the Word Band was to go to the next step of using vocal arrangements to perform poetry. Of course, this group has to be heard to be appreciated, and plans are underway to release two or three selections by The Word Band as part of a projected CD whose working title is *New Orleans Soirée*: A Gathering Of The Saints / Kalamu ya Salaam & Friends. *Saints* is a collaborative recording of me working with New Orleans musicians in a wide variety of musical contexts, ranging from a piece called "Congo Square" performed with Percussion Inc. to totally improvised poetry performed with Kidd Jordan and Alvin Fielder's avant garde ensemble, The Improvisational Arts Quintet. Other musicians are blues guitarist Walter Washington; legendary traditional jazz banjoist, guitarist and vocalist Danny Barker; saxophonist Tim Green; and a cameo by my brother, trumpeter Kenneth Ferdinand.

I had also developed a working relationship with Chinese American Fred Ho, a baritone saxophonist, composer and political activist. We called our collaboration the Afro Asian Arts Dialogue. We did a tour through Michigan, also performing at the Nuyorican Theatre in New York City, at Brandeis University, in Atlanta, and at the University of Madison, Wisconsin. Recordings were made of our performances in New York and Madison.

My intention is to release this work in recorded form because I know that the fullest appreciation of poetry in the oral tradition will not happen unless and until it is heard. This necessarily requires getting into the "business" of recording poetry. Although there are a few publishing houses who regularly record poets, there are no companies currently specializing in producing, recording, and distributing African American poetry.

I have served an apprenticeship in the recording business by working as a producer with All For One Records (AFO), a small, independent jazz label founded by Harold Battiste. So I have the experience but lack an infrastructure and necessary capital.

This is also a major part of my problem: I have the demonstrated ability to fulfill a variety of required functions. I am not only a writer; I am also an entrepreneur, an administrator, an arts producer, a radio personality and a father of five. Each of those areas has its own sphere of influence and expertise, and I find myself very often pulled away from my writing and editing work to function in another area. How else could it be?

Creating, producing, and preserving our poetry is really not the hardest part of our struggle, however. The most difficult step is developing a theory and critique of what we are trying to accomplish.

In my office there is a portrait of Amílcar Cabral, whom I mentioned earlier on, which I obtained in Cuba. It was Cabral's seminal essay "National Liberation and Culture" that opened the theoretical way ahead for me. I quote Cabral's "aims of cultural resistance" as they are the basic framework that I use to define my own cultural work:

> Development of a people's culture and of all aboriginal positive cultural values
>
> Development of a national culture on the basis of history and the conquests of the struggle itself
>
> Constant raising of the political and moral awareness of the people (of all social categories) and of patriotism, spirit of sacrifice and devotion to the cause of independence, justice and progress
>
> Development of the technical and technological scientific culture, compatible with the demands of progress

> Development, on the basis of a critical assimilation of mankind's conquests in the domains of art, science, literature, etc., of a universal culture, aiming at perfect integration in the contemporary world and its prospects for evolution
>
> Constant and generalized raising of feelings of humanism, solidarity, respect and disinterested devotion to the human being.

Based on my study of Cabral, I advocate the importance of cultural specificity, cultural integrity, and the legitimacy of cultural accretion.

Cultural specificity reflects itself in the need to be grounded as an artist. One must really know one's culture (whether native or adopted). Being grounded (i.e., "knowing your culture") is not anthropological but rather is a commitment to the study, propagation and perpetuation of the culture "as a citizen of that culture." In this way, culture is not simply an object of observation but rather is also a mode of subjective operation—is not something one studies outside of the self but rather is a way of living which defines the self.

Part of my struggle as a writer was to both learn and project New Orleans culture. In my work there were three ways to use the specificity of New Orleans culture: one, as content, two, as style, and three, as a structural model. Although content is an obvious approach, and although I have written a large body of prose which focuses on New Orleans, I have very few poems that "image" New Orleans as a geo-cultural space. Indeed, the majority of my poems that reference New Orleans are praise poems for specific cultural figures. Given my oral orientation, it is understandable that my use of New Orleans culture would lean more toward style and structure.

Cultural integrity requires an honest assessment of strengths and weaknesses plus a genuine acceptance of one's cultural identity. One cannot hope to preserve or project cultural integrity if one a) objectively does not know and understand one's culture and b) has not accepted that one's culture is a legitimate and valuable expression of human culture. Especially for African Americans, who live in both physical and psychological proximity to a dominant and dominating culture, accepting the legitimacy of African American culture is not easy.

A word about "knowing" African American culture: none of us truly know our culture because so much of our culture is unknowable. This is true precisely because our culture has been destroyed, dispersed, masked, and disrupted. Indeed, those of us who champion African American culture are actually championing the reclamation, reconstruction, and reevaluation of that culture. All the surface aspects we talk about are just that: surface.

For example, no matter how much we claim to "love" Black music, how can we be champions of our culture when we have done so few studies of our music? To the truism that one could tell "how Black" an intellectual was by looking at her or his library, I used to respond with my own saying: if you really want to know "how Black" (meaning "how cultured") an intellectual is, check out their record collection. Why? Because our culture has been recorded but not written. Because books may be assigned in school, but records you generally buy on your own based on your own tastes, whatever they may be—and here I am not elevating one genre of Great Black Music over another. I mean quite simply that the embracing of our music is a sine qua non of embracing our culture.

At the same time, I must recognize that "our" music is essentially American music in the totality of its expression, even though the core of it equals the creation of African American culture. We are both African and American. As paradoxical as it may sound, Elvis Presley, Country&Western, hard rock, all of those examples of American music are entwined in and cannot be separated from the core elements that African Americans created. There is no one more American than African Americans, even as there is also no one in America as African as African Americans and African immigrants—all of this analysis itself being an example of cultural integrity in practice.

Third, we must move forward and recognize that cultural accretions are not only inevitable, they are also essential. Accretionizing is a seminal force for Afrocentric cultures in general, and African American culture specifically is an "American" culture, which means that it is a "Creole" culture. Our strains are various, and even though some of us may be eastbound, the west is nevertheless in us.

The concept of cultural accretions helped me to put my high school experiences at St. Aug in proper perspective. My initial memories, as discussed earlier, are full of anger and rejection. But those initial memories are not wholly factual; in fact, they are self-serving. I hated the goals of St. Aug, but emotionally I both loved and hated St. Aug and all it stood for.

I was a Baptist, so there was a conflict of religious beliefs, but more important than that, I was working class oriented by social experience and by ideological commitment. St. Aug's agenda was to create the talented tenth: doctors, lawyers, politicians, scientists. Most of my fellow students did not share my civil rights activism—yet I was influenced by them. I played ball and went to parties with them. I could not fail to be impressed by their intelligence (actually their "education," rather than native intelligence).

My first true love, Thelma Thomas, was a physician's daughter. One of my best friends at St. Aug, Emile LaBranche, was the son of a pharmacist. They all lived in a very different part of New Orleans than me. Many of these classmates were Creoles, and the physical differences between the neighborhoods where we lived were analogous to the differences between Black and White neighborhoods in other cities. My rejection of St. Aug was partially a reaction to that world's rejection of my world and partially my own inability to understand the dual attraction and repulsion I felt for the lifestyle of Black professionals.

All of the psychological turmoil notwithstanding, St. Aug gave me intellectual tools that were denied most of the people who lived where I lived. Later, in FST and in Ahidiana, the educational differences among members were obstacles with which we had to struggle mightily. At Ahidiana we called it "uneven levels of development." As I read more and more of Fanon and Cabral—especially Cabral with his work on the "class suicide" of the petit bourgeoisie in the context of revolutionary struggle, and also his conceptualizations of "returning to the source" to define the integration of the professionals into the ranks of the masses—it all became clearer to me. I was then more able to understand the conflicts and separate the wheat from the chaff in those experiences.

While I never did get a four-year college education, my ability to read and write was clearly superior to most of the people in my neighborhood as a child and superior to many of the people with whom I shared civil rights and Black power/Black liberation struggles. Although certainly neither created nor ideologically defined by St. Aug, my reading and writing skills were qualitatively enhanced by having a strong college preparatory curriculum in high school.

There are all kinds of dimensions to this question. Suffice it to say, Cabral gave me the intellectual tools to appreciate the accretion of my own educational history.

* * *

To some, none of this has anything to do with creating poetry. To me it has everything to do with creating an authentic African American poetry. Paradoxically, my codification of a Black aesthetic made significant leaps while working in haiku, a foreign form.

Haiku is a Japanese poetry form which structurally consists of three lines and a total of seventeen syllables (five on the first and third lines and seven on the second line). Once I began writing in haiku, I wanted to figure out how to incorporate an African American aesthetic into that form.

For me this was more than simply a technical question of how to write it on paper; it was also a question of how to perform haiku. I would not consider myself successful until I had figured out how to recite haiku with the same force as I did my blues and jazz-based poetry.

I knew I had to deal with at least three different elements: rhythm, rhyme and sound—plus, they needed to carry the weight of irony. Of course, I did not expect each poem to contain every element, but I was striving to have each poem manifest at least one of those properties. I did not study any traditional haiku nor read any books on writing haiku; I wanted to use the form in my own way.

This was a left brain/right brain problem. I needed a creative approach for the performance and a technical approach for the writing. I stored it away and let my subconscious work on the performance part.

The writing part was easy once I focused on what I wanted to do. Eventually I moved away from similes and went straight into personifications. I made the natural world an extension of the human self. I used imagery but also dealt with the Afrocentric tradition of proverbs, mother wit and "mama say." I used alliteration, rhyme and rhythm. I wanted to reach for Creolization, bringing together concepts that were not usually thought of as part of a whole. Beneath all of that I wanted to maintain a feminine/masculine referencing.

Haiku #97 is a good example.

haiku #97

i enter your church,
you receive my offerings,
our screaming choirs merge

It's written in three with the emphasis on ONE-TWO-three. The "three" is an open beat, meaning I could recite it ONE-TWO-three or ONE-TWO-three/three/three/three-ONE-TWO-three. Usually, I recite it rubato, without any particular rhythmic emphasis, but I keep the three feel in mind so that the words are emphasized like this:

I EN-TER your church
YOU RE-CEIVE my offering
OUR SCREAM-MING choirs mergeeeeee.

Unfortunately, there is nothing on the page that can tell you how I am using rhythm except that I have set the poem up with the emphatic words at the beginning of each line. Additionally, each line opens with two words; the first word is one syllable, and the second word is two syllables, which is also a reinforcement of the three feel, but it's a three within the first two counts of the larger three.

Here is a haiku that leans heavily on the use of the "ssss" sound contrasted against the abruptness of the terminal "t" sound.

haiku #37

savoring the flesh
of your kiss, i chew sun &
spit out midnight stars

The rhythm break is like this:

Sa-vo-RINGGG/the-flesh
of-your KISSSS, i-chew SUNNN
and-spit (pause) / out
mid-Night STARSSSS

Once again, I'm using three.

Here is a more ambitious piece. I wanted to write about sadness, the breaking up of one into two separate pieces. I wanted to capture the feel of separation. I use rhyme ("gone/flown/song/sung" are all half rhymes) and rhythm (the middle line sets up an interesting swing with the use of the "s" sound repeated five times within seven syllables), as well as image. The image alone would have been sufficient for the idea of the poem, but the rhyme and rhythm add the Afrocentric. In this selection the last word, "harmony," which is three syllables long, contrasts quite unharmoniously with all the preceding words which are either one or two syllables long; in other words, it's ironically the word "harmony" that breaks the poem's rhythmic unity.

haiku #123

love gone is bird flown
sad sunset song tartly sung
without harmony

Haiku #48 is what I call a "perfect" haiku, meaning it has exactly seventeen words *and* seventeen syllables. This haiku is also an example of using blues imagery, being a direct variation on the blues line "fattening frogs for snakes." I personify the night, the quality of hurt, and then use a simile to make complete the blues reference.

haiku #48

night moans grip my waist
the arms of hurt snake round me,
i feel like a frog

Of course, I also from time to time infused my haiku with specifically Black content. Here is a piece which has a rather involved origin. The basic line is taken from Ho Chi Minh, who wrote "when the prison doors fly open / the dragons fly out" referring to political prisoners. I had learned that Ho Chi Minh lived for a brief time in Harlem and had been influenced by Marcus Garvey. When Nelson Mandela was released from prison, I wanted to capture the feel of that. Upon seeing Mr. Mandela step into the sunlight, what immediately struck me was the beauty of his smile. Also, Malcolm X and George Jackson approached prison as a school. I had read about imprisoned ANC militants also approaching captivity as a school. The implied cocoon is the school. Finally, it occurred to me that the whole process was one of transformation. So, I wrote this haiku.

haiku #112 ***(for Mandela)***

emerging from jail
their dragon/our butterfly
his smile is so huge

I was well on the road to using haiku as text, but I still had to figure out how to make haiku work as speech. I believe the answer probably came to me when I heard a musical selection that reminded me of an Art Ensemble of Chicago (AEC) concert I'd experienced in Atlanta. The AEC performed one number entirely on large bamboo flutes with shimmering gongs in the background. There was an incredible quality of tranquility achieved by using long, low extended notes. I had already mastered the ability to mimic musical instruments, and the key was to figure out how to achieve that feeling/sound. I tried and tried and eventually was able to achieve a sound similar to a bass flute but not quite as mellow as the big bamboo flute.

Once I had the sound, I figured then I could improvise the words in the sense of repeating them, extending them, and repeating phrases, in-between blowing the flute notes. The key is to get inside the sound completely. There is no set melody. No set rhythms. I use however I am feeling at the moment, close my eyes and listen to my breathing. As I begin reciting sometimes it takes a minute to begin, sometimes longer. Generally I cannot do more than two or three haiku at a time because it takes so much energy. But I had figured it out.

The test, of course, was to perform it. It works!

There is another component. I use microphone techniques I learned not only from performing but also from radio work. I know how to blow across, next to, and into a microphone so that the noise of the air mixes with the sounds/words emanating from my larynx to form the total sound of the haiku presentation. At one point, I wondered could I do it without a microphone. The answer was yes, as long as I was in a small room and was very close to the audience.

What I had previously done in the long form, in the blues and jazz forms, I could now achieve in the haiku form—I was close to figuring out a theory of Black poetics.

I already knew that I had to have an audience and that poetry had to be orated. Working with the haiku gave me a missing part: how to put the aesthetics into the text so that the piece could stand on its own as text and, at the same time, serve as lyric for the ultimate oration of the selection.

* * *

I have been working on this for the last five years. Experimenting. Studying. Talking with other poets. Actually, I have been working on this for many, many years; it's just that over the last five years I have been focused. Why? On the one hand, reciting poetry was easy. But explaining what I was doing and how I did it was not so easy. I wanted to be able to articulate the theory as well as articulate the poem.

Moreover, I understood that there was a need to compete in the arena of text. I was clear that if my poetry was going to be published by people other than myself—a departure from the ethos of Adihana and BLKARTSOUTH—then it had to achieve viability on the page and be able to stand up as text in comparison to most English poetry. I wanted to create a body of poetry that would make a contribution to the African American literary tradition. I was not in search of popularity—what I wanted, and have always wanted, was relevance. The difference is now I view relevance not in the present tense but rather in the continuum.

Tom Dent articulates a belief that I share: our most important audience may in fact be in the future, those who will find antecedent and inspiration in the work that we do. I want to posit poetry worthy of that audience's perusal and study. This is a major shift in my thinking. I have moved from immediate feedback from our contemporary community as validation. I now believe the validation of our work comes not solely from the community as it currently exists but also from the community as it existed in the past and as I think/hope it will exist in the future.

How does one receive validation from the past? By consciously incorporating the tradition and keeping alive the spirit of the ancestors. How does one receive validation from the future? By consciously creating cradles that will support future efforts.

I go back to Langston Hughes. It is not enough just to write poetry. I must also gather and uphold the dispersed work of early poets (many of whom were overlooked in their time much like many of us are overlooked now). I must close the circle, reconstruct the calabash. I must dare to care about my ancestors and make a fitting home for them within whatever contemporary space I call home because "my home" is not truly home unless and until my ancestors are there with me. At some point, we must understand that "caring" for our history is also a creative act.

The Western notion of "self" (in general and of the artist in particular) as an autonomous individual is what we are struggling against. When I collect and cause to be printed (or recorded) the works of ancestor poets, I have, in the collective sense, written poetry.

This is why in 1990 I edited, and, in conjunction with Felton Eaddy, produced *WORD UP: Black Poetry Of The 80s From The Deep South*. That anthology featured sixty-seven poems by forty (evenly divided female/male) poets, representing each of the nine Deep South states excluding Alabama and Arkansas.

In my introduction, I addressed both the question of "poetry" per se and the rationale behind the title. Listen:

> Poetry is a revealer. And a connector. By revealing the essence of us, our differences as well as our commonalities, poetry makes it possible for us to know our individual selves, our collective selves, and also know others on a visceral level through the power and impact of art.
>
> At the gut level, the only substitute for firsthand experience is art. Quality poetry emotionally connects us to the world—it both helps the world "know" and, hopefully, understand us while simultaneously and dialectically helping us to know and understand the world. When the poet is really poeting, the poet becomes the voice of our heart as well as the window on the souls of others.
>
> While it is important to look out on the world, we also desperately need to understand ourselves, our condition, and, yes, our slavery nurtured psychosis—it is painful to realize how well we aren't. Our art helps us recognize and cope with both our negatives and our positives.
>
> Though this recognition of the reality of our condition might be unpleasant at times, rather than papering over these differences, art delves deeply into them. Great art is always specific, always telling in how well it details the interior lives of those who create the art and those who are the subject matter of the art.
>
> Although African Americans are one people, there are contradictions and differences among us, especially now that the great leveler of segregation has been lifted slightly. The gender gap, or the age gap, or the class gap

is sometimes so wide that often only the mediation of art enables us to make the connection between where we are and where our sister or brother is.

Only after we actually feel the difference, only then can the majority of us even begin to feel what the other feels, and only after making the emotional connection can we earnestly commit ourselves to building community and closing the gap between us. Art enables us to care about others, others whom we might otherwise ignore.

But beyond that, we are dealing with another need. This anthology is for those of us who not only love and recognize the connective potency of poetry but indeed, who actually need poetry to survive. Although music is generally considered the sine qua non of African American life, there is no contradiction in elevating poetry to the level of music because, from our perspective, poetry, which is the music of spoken language, is just another way to sing.

Listen some more:

> We decided on the name WORD UP because it implied not only an (re)ascension of the Afrocentric aesthetic, the very name WORD UP also reverberates on the term "Word."
>
> "Word" is both a popular expression of the 80s and a concept of historic resonance for African Americans. Most of our people are familiar with the concept of "word" from the Bible (as in: "in the beginning was the word and the word was God"). But there is also the racial memory of traditional African concepts such as "nommo," which find their new world corollary in the concept of "word."
>
> Additionally, by saying "Up" we not only implied that we were coming "up out of the South," we also implied that we were attempting to raise the WORD to a higher level.

> So, thus we created WORD UP as an effort to provide exposure for and to display the works of African American poets who were working in the Deep South, and who also, consciously or unconsciously, espoused an Afrocentric aesthetic sense, which bases their work in the day to day lives, loves and aspirations of working class African Americans. Although we did not impose any aesthetical or political guidelines, most of the poets who responded, clearly adhere to this perspective.

Compare the "sound" of the introduction to *WORD UP* with the sound of the pieces quoted from *Nkombo*. I do not disavow nor repudiate those earlier works. I am simply speaking now from a different place, sounding what I see and suggesting that while the objectives are approximately the same as we had in the past, and while the subject remains the same, the song/sound itself has been deepened by carrying the weight of experience.

There were several pieces that served as my major springboard in focusing on Afrocentric language as text. One was an interview I did with Toni Cade Bambara, which was published in Vol. 2 No. 4 (1980) issue of *First World*:

> FIRST WORLD: Are you consciously trying to do anything in particular with your style of writing?
>
> TONI CADE BAMBARA: I'm trying to learn how to write! I think there have been a lot of things going on in the Black experience for which there are no terms, certainly not in English at this moment. There are a lot of aspects of consciousness for which there is no vocabulary, no structure in the English language which would allow people to validate that experience through the language. I'm trying to find a way to do that.

> FW: Do you see yourself, then, essentially in search of a language?
>
> TCB: That's one of the things I'm trying to do.
>
> FW: Why hasn't this happened before? Do you think other writers have tried to do this and been unsuccessful?
>
> TCB: I don't know. I do know that the English language that grew from European languages has been systematically stripped of the kinds of structures and the kinds of vocabularies that allow people to plug into other kinds of intelligences. That's no secret. That's part of their whole history, wherein people cannot be a higher sovereign than the state. At the time when wise folk were put to the rack was also a time when books were burned, temples razed to the ground, and certain types of language "mysteries"—for lack of a better word—were suppressed. That's the legacy of the West.
>
> I'm just trying to tell the truth, and I think in order to do that we will have to invent, in addition to new forms, new modes and new idioms. I think we will have to connect language in that kind of way. I don't know yet what that is.

The second part of the article on Toni, the commentary, is a cogent summation of the quest for language:

> Achieving a written language is not simply about duplication, or even "replication," of the language we hear in our communities and neighborhoods. Because, like our music, as of this moment there is no adequate form of written notation which can fully render our sound to paper. The struggle of the committed African-American writer is to create the written forms which can adequately translate

the reality and visions, the past, present and hoped for future, into black and white on a page.

In an effort to give "currency" to our mother tongue and its "folksy" essence, some of our writers have taken to attempting to write in a way that mimics or mirrors African-American speech. This process, at one time called "dialect," is characteristic not only of African-American literature, but also characteristic of most of the literature of African peoples who have been colonialized in the Western hemisphere whenever diasporan-African writers attempted to give voice to or be the voice of the particular people from which they originate.

In the U.S.A. the most frequently cited paradigm of this process and style of writing was the "Negro" verse of Paul L. Dunbar. During the Sixties, trying to get down to it, we would "be" dropping g's and adopting a ditty-bopping style which was better understood and appreciated when heard than simply read. The elliptical spelling and speech-like patterns of Ntozake Shange are probably the best known examples of Seventies dialect writing. But words change, sounds change, tempo, rhythm and the gestures associated with talk, all of that changes and, thus, I suggest that "dialect" alone has only a surface relationship to the actual quest for the mother tongue, for an African-American language.

In the Caribbean and in Central and South America, this process, the use of "dialect," generally is referred to as using the local "patois." The patois is generally the Africanization of the colonial language. What is sometimes referred to as "Black English" is actually African-American patois.

In a context within which the use of African languages was strictly forbidden (either de jure or de facto) and actively discouraged by force, our people's use of patois reflects, not, as has been mistaken by some, the attempt of the ignorant and illiterate to speak the English (or French or Spanish or Portuguese) language; rather, the significance of patois is that it reflects the will of our people to inject our African root and essence into everything we do and say, and especially into the way we communicate with each other. Patois, in our case "Black English," is not the bastard tongue of aliens and slaves imitating the master. Patois is the affirmation of the African presence in the Western hemisphere.

Furthermore, language is not just style, it is not only "how" we say or write something. What makes one language fundamentally different from another is not how it sounds, but indeed, its actual "structure," which is derived from the users' worldview, i.e., how the users of the language view themselves, other people and the world. The creation of any language which is fundamentally different in worldview from the colonial language is the most subversive act, short of actual revolution, that any colonized people can conceive and carry out.

Unfortunately, most of us who are literate in the colonial tongue, especially those of us who are nonpolitical or apolitical oriented writers, have generally failed to understand the importance of establishing the mother tongue. Too many of us as writers have spent unretrievable time attempting to demonstrate that we had mastered the colonial language. Thus, much of our "writing" has an "outside" quality vis-à-vis our own people. We write from the outside looking in, we write as an observer/voyeur who is explaining to others (those who are equally "literate" in the colonial language) what these "people," our own people, are all about. It is essentially a pimp/peephole act/art.

In fact, the very act of writing and publishing in the post-chattel slavery period is often considered a sign that some writer has "made it," i.e. collaborated with and been accepted by the colonial master.

As I've expressed, a major part of my search has not been for Afrocentric content but for structure and style, and this is no simple thing—particularly since my search has been couched in poetry as opposed to prose. Prose is the everyday written usage of language susceptible to "common," as well as specialized, influences. Prose is also less literary than poetry in the sense that prose as a totality is not claimed as the province of the elite.

This was not always the case, particularly in those historic eras when writing in toto was the province of a special class. Yet, prose was democratic in the history of writing in America precisely because industry cannot do without prose. They needed manuals and minutes of meetings, records of transactions and logs detailing merchandise, discoveries, exploits and military operations. Why else was the slave narrative possible? Why not slave poems?

If you are interested, look at how many more critical texts have been written about African American prose as compared to the relatively small number of critical texts written about African American poetry. Critical consideration indicates acceptance by the intelligentsia—and so Black poetry remains relatively rejected, further enhancing prose's democratic profile.

Prose is also more open to experimentation; hence, we have the magic realism of Latin America or the *Memories of Fire* American history trilogy by Eduardo Galeano. Jean Toomer, his use of iambic pentameter aside, eschewed a Eurocentric style and embraced the patois when he wrote the prose of *Cane*. But poetry, on the other hand, because it is a distillation of language, is the most codified, considered more specialized. The poetic text is the last bastion of Eurocentric linguistic domination—just as my pre-Langston early conceptions of poetry reflected.

After Toni Cade Bambara, the second influence in contemplating Afrocentric language as text was Barbadian poet/historian Edward Kamau Brathwaite, the person whom I once considered the greatest living poet in the Western hemisphere. Period. In the the early eighties I did this short interview with Brathwaite.

SALAAM: What are you trying to do with your poetry now?

BRATHWAITE: My poetry has been concerned, for a long time now, with the attempt to reconstruct in verse, in metric and in rhythms, the nature of the culture of the people of the Caribbean. This involves not only discovering what I would call "new poetic forms"—a breakaway from the English pentameter—but also, and more importantly, discovering the nature of our folk culture, the myths, the legends, the speech rhythms, the way we express ourselves in words, the way we express ourselves in song. That has been my concern for about ten years and is increasingly so. One has to develop technical resources of a very complex nature, and at the same time one has to get an increasing knowledge of who our people are, where they come from and the nature of their soul.

SALAAM: What's so important about that?

BRATHWAITE: Well, what's important is that until we can do that we remain "ex-selves"; we remain nobodies; we remain just imitations of those who had colonized us. Considering that the man in the street, our own people, the common man has always been himself, it is ridiculous that the artists have remained a shadow of that self. What we have to do now is to increasingly bring the artist and the people together.

SALAAM: Do you prefer working on the page, or would you like to do more recordings?

BRATHWAITE: Both. I wouldn't separate them. My poems start off as rhythms in my head, as patterns of songs that also have an objective. The patterns of songs have to say something, address themselves to some problems or go through some dialectical process. From my head they have to be transferred onto the page because that's how I started, but then from the page I instinctively transfer it on to song. In other words, every time I write a poem, I have to either have it read or read it myself to some kind of audience before I'm satisfied that it's a real poem. The recordings are a necessary part of the whole process.

SALAAM: What's the importance of the audience in that process?

BRATHWAITE: The audience gives me feedback. The audience completes the circle. The audience are the people I'm writing about and for, and therefore, if they can't understand what I'm saying, it means that it might be that I've failed. There are some cases where I think I'm ahead of the audience, but then I would know that, and they would know it too, but you've got to start from a base that the audience and yourself agree on and move from there.

SALAAM: Who is this audience that you speak of? Obviously you don't just mean people in general..

BRATHWAITE: I start off with a Caribbean audience, which is representative of the people who have been down-pressed. The audience is usually a mixed audience, moving in terms of class from college educated to middle class right up to the laboring class because that is how our society is composed.

SALAAM: What immediate reactions do you find valuable as verification, and what long range reactions do you find valuable as verification?

BRATHWAITE: The immediate reactions are one of ascent or descent. You can tell from face and feeling, body movement, if you are saying the right thing. That is clear. But the long-range reaction is very interesting. I'll give you an example: I'm starting to use a lot of possession (religious) sequences in my work. Because the work is culturally accurate, instinctively when people come to it, they want to perform it; they don't just want to read it. Nearly all my work in the Caribbean is done as a performance with groups. Now, a young group of actors recently came into contact with my latest poem, which was essentially involved with religion, native religion, Afro-Caribbean religion. They were not themselves fully aware of what I was talking about, but they could tell from the descriptions, the external aspects of the descriptions, the kinds of churches I was talking about. They went to those churches in order to experience for themselves what was happening, and many of them have now become members of those churches. As artists they find themselves now being fulfilled as members of those people's churches. I think that's a very significant long-term effect because it is really motivating people not just to talk about their culture but to become participants in its root basis. The Haitians have done it too. The Haitians are increasingly returning to vodun as a central experience. With the African person, the religion is the center of the culture; therefore every artist, at some stage, must become rootedly involved in a religious complexity.

SALAAM: How do you deal with the mystification inherent in much of the religion?

BRATHWAITE: It is not mystification at all; that's the thing about it. The religion is so natural, it is so vital, it is so socially oriented, so people oriented that there is no

> mysticism—mental mystification—in it at all. That is really the difference between an African-oriented religion and a European one. Theirs is very mystified because they are not dealing with a living god; they're not dealing with man in relation to god in relation to community.
>
> SALAAM: They're not people centered.
>
> BRATHWAITE: Right. In the African sense the religion is medicine; it is philosophy; it is martial arts; it is everything, holistic.
>
> SALAAM: In that sense the work you are doing is people-centered work as opposed to idea centered?
>
> BRATHWAITE: Right. As opposed to art-centered work, art for art's sake.

From a vision outside the U.S.A. but inside the African Diaspora, Brathwaite grapples with the same text and language issues I have grappled with throughout my life. While I agree with the overall tenor of what he said, I think he avoids dealing with the "blues," which is simply our response to the denial of our humanity by humans more powerful than both we and our traditional god(s). Brathwaite is not a "practicing" member of any particular organized religious group; he locates the center of religion in the people orientation. This is an avoidance of the most troubling question: why did our old gods fail us, what did we do to deserve our lot, to be(come) so Black and blue?

We reenter the question raised much earlier in this writing. There is a schism between the blues folk and the religious (particularly the Christians). I agree with Brathwaite that there must be a religious center, spiritual beliefs—but I do not believe that presupposes organized religions, whether Christian or Islamic. A central (and, some would say, existential) question ultimately must be addressed by every serious writer who confronts African American culture: the failure of "God" (religion) to provide earthly deliverance.

In search of the answer I went back to the beginning, to the core, to the people, and placed my faith in them and in nature, in what I can witness and in what created me, thus:

haiku #58

black people believe
in god, and i believe in
black people, amen

Ultimately, every African American poet worth her or his salt must address in one way or another, directly or indirectly, bluntly or subtly, this most basic of all questions: how come we must suffer so? Regardless of the specific answer posed or the specific solution suggested, I believe such wrestling is an essential characteristic of the Black aesthetic and is also the source of our characteristic melancholic tinge which colors, to one degree or another, every African American gesture.

My understanding of the phenomenology of Black poetry was further uplifted by Kamau Brathwaite through an instructive lecture published in text form as *History of the Voice*. In terms of explicating the structure of his poetic language and relating that language to the liberation struggle, Brathwaite had gone further than any poet I knew. Brathwaite's work has parallels in the work of some linguists, but the difference is: Brathwaite was dealing with the inherent revolutionary nature of Black expressive voice in the face of colonial domination, a paradigm which remains profoundly applicable today.

Brathwaite defines "nation language" thusly:

> ...National language is the language which is influenced very strongly by the African model, the African aspect of

our New World/Caribbean heritage. English it may be in terms of some of its lexical features. But in its contours, its rhythm and timbre, its sound explosions, it is not English, even though the words, as you hear them, might be English to a greater or lesser degree."

[. . .]

Now I'd like to describe for you some of the characteristics of our nation language. First of all, it is from, as I've said, an oral tradition. The poetry, the culture itself, exists not in a dictionary but in the tradition of the spoken word. It is based as much on sound as it is on song. That is to say, the noise that it makes is part of the meaning, and if you ignore the noise (or what you would think of as noise, shall I say) then you or lose part of the meaning. When it is written, you lose the sound or the noise, and therefore you lose part of the meaning. Which is, again, why I have to have a tape recorder for this presentation. I want you to get the sound of it, rather than the sight of it.

In order to break down the pentameter, we discovered an ancient form which was always there, the calypso. This is a form that I think nearly everyone knows about. It does not employ the iambic pentameter. It employs dactyls. It therefore mandates the use of the tongue in a certain way, the use of sound in a certain way. It is a model that we are moving naturally towards now. Compare

To be or not to be, that is the question

The stone had skidded arc'd and bloomed into islands
Cuba San Domingo
Jamaica Puerto Rico

> But not only is there a different in syllabic or stress pattern, there is an important difference in shape of intonation. In the Shakespeare, the voice travels in a single forward plane towards the horizon of its end. In the kaiso, after the skimming movement of the first line, we have a distinct variation. The voice dips and deepens to describe an intervallic pattern. And then there are more ritual forms like kumina, like shango, the religious forms, which I won't have time to go into here, but which begin to disclose the complexity that is possible with nation language.
>
> The other thing about nation language is that it is part of what may be called total expression, a notion which is not unfamiliar to you because you are coming back to that kind of thing now. Reading is an isolated, individualistic expression. The oral tradition on the other hand demands not only the griot but the audience to complete the community: the noise and sounds that the maker makes are responded to by the audience and are returned to him. Hence we have the creation of a continuum where meaning truly resides. And this total expression comes about because people be in the open air, because people live in conditions of poverty ('unhouselled') because they come from a historical experience where they had to rely on their very breath rather than on paraphernalia like books and museums and machines. They had to depend on immanence, the power within themselves, rather than the technology outside themselves.

What was important for me is that Brathwaite had clearly articulated not only structural differences but also the social basis for those differences. When I put Brathwaite's insights with Zora Neal Hurston's remarks about "Negro Expression," the shape of the poetry I wanted and needed to create became clear.

Zora Hurston's essay is at once a timeless meditation on the nature of why and how we express ourselves, as well as a period piece obviously grounded in (but not limited by) the "slang" of her era:

> Very few Negroes, educated or not, use a clear clipped "I." It verges more or less upon "Ah." I think the lip form is responsible for this to a great extent. By experiment the reader will find that a sharp "i" is very much easier with a thin taut lip than with a full soft lip. Like tightening violin strings."

Zora's ruminations opened a number of doors of inner insight for me, especially when set in the framework constructed by Brathwaite. In essence, Zora Hurston advised me to study our people, totally and without shame. While I don't fully subscribe to her worldview, I do appreciate the fact that she used her people, embodied and whole, as a basis for developing her ideas.

* * *

Well before I could intellectually articulate my theory of a Black aesthetic, I had already accepted the basic tenets—a blues inheritance, a multivalent conception of blackness, an interdependence between the individual and the collective voice—because I loved the music of John Coltrane.

My love of Coltrane was not instantaneous; in fact, early on I would walk out of the room when Coltrane came on the Saturday evening jazz radio program. But there was something that pulled me into Trane's sound. Eventually, I realized "that woman" was in his horn, i.e., Trane was a profound blues musician. In him, once again I heard the cry of the blues, a cry that was both brutally raw in its sound and sophisticated in its articulation.

My ultimately successful efforts to feel, embrace, and understand Coltrane intellectually stimulated and spiritually focused my development of Afrocentric literary theories. Throughout my life, music has always preceded intellectual discovery. The sound of the music would grab me well before I could make sense out of the structure and sophisticated articulation of both the country blues singers and the modern jazz musicians.

Modern jazz moved me to think, particularly John Coltrane. In modern jazz, Coltrane reintroduced blues as the dominant emotional vector as well as the conceptual structure of his music. Afterwards, he began incorporating both spirituals/gospel and world musics in his work. Finally, he added a spiritual dimension to his work by proposing that we are all one and all part of a much larger life force. Coltrane articulated key aspects of his philosophy in conversation with Nat Hentoff, who wrote the liner notes for Coltrane's path-breaking release *Meditations*.

> Once you become aware of this force for unity in life, you can't ever forget it. It becomes part of everything you do. In that respect, this is an extension of *A Love Supreme* since my conception of that force keeps changing shape. My goal in meditating on this through music, however, remains the same. And that is to uplift people, as much as I can. To inspire them to realize more and more of their capacities for living meaningful lives. Because there certainly is meaning to life.

The awesome inclusiveness of Trane's music—a sound at once informed by the world yet unmistakably and unalterably Black—suggested to me the possibility of a non-separatist approach to Afrocentrism. His music was like the sun, radiating ideas (shooting them out to investigate the depths of the universe) and at the same time gravitationally so strong that it pulled an entire galaxy into orbit around itself. Any question I could pose, the music had already addressed. Every answer I would achieve, the music had prepared me to accept. By 1992 I had begun formalizing my approach, or as the musicians would say: I had found my sound.

What is interesting here is that although much of my work, particularly the oral, was immediately identifiable, the sound I had was not the sound I was reaching to attain. Again, the music was instructive. Jazz is generally created in a collective but simultaneously always celebrates the individual. In the best jazz combos, one can tell who each musician is just by hearing their own unique sound, yet it is paradoxical that an individual sound is developed by playing with others, never in isolation—even though the isolation of shedding is necessary to developing craft and technique.

But technique is not sound. That is why Thelonious Monk, for instance, is immediately identifiable as a pianist even though he did not have the technical abilities of many pianists of lesser importance to the music.

All of these kinds of considerations are reflected in my poetry. While I spent years experimenting and performing, writing and rewriting, refashioning and/or jettisoning old ideas and techniques, discovering new ones and adopting others, through all of that I knew that ultimately it was about being myself. I had to find out who I was and had to articulate the truths that I found.

Eventually, I also understood that, if I were successful, not only would I create my own sound, I would also create my own sense. Like Black musicians have for hundreds of years, I would learn by reflection and projection, reflecting on myself and the world, projecting what I had discovered. I would have my own sound, and I would conceive my own sense of what my life was about. This revelation is best expressed in a short poem contained in *What Is Life*, a collection of poetry and essays published by Third World Press in 1994.

The Meaning Of Life

sometimes I sit
    and I wonder
    what is the meaning
    of life
I sit
sometimes
and I wonder
    and then I realize
    I am the meaning
    of my own life
the meaning is me

In June of 1994 I finished a collection of love poetry titled *I Enter Your Church*. Containing a poem written in 1965 and including many others written over a two-decade period, this collection has a range that none of my previous poetry collections were able to reach precisely because I am now consciously working from a conscious aesthetic structure.

To create what I call revolutionary Black art within a dominant and dominating White supremacist culture requires me as an African American artist to develop a consciousness that strives for the purity of artistic expression, rather than an uncritical and unartistic reversion to raw expression. All artists must study if their work is to move beyond naive expressionism into modernity. We can certainly be without embracing the modern, but modernity presupposes being; and paradoxically, whether we embrace modernity or not, we are psychologically shaped by our modern context.

What is the difference between modernity and naivete? Modernity is reflective while naivete is reflexive. Modernity thinks before it acts. Naivete acts simply as it feels.

Whatever the objective—whether the study of history or the creation of a revolution, whether collaboration with the dominant forces or construction of iconoclastic alternatives—whatever we do will inevitably be done in the present (or, as Charlie Parker said on his horn, "Now Is The Time"), a "time" defined by modernity. Inspired by the examples of Coltrane, Cabral, Bambara, Brathwaite, Baraka, Jones, Baldwin, Hughes, and literally hundreds of others, I have fashioned my own individual response to the problems posed by living in these modern times: how to move Black(ly) into the future.

There are numerous examples of great naive art in the fields of music and dance, but that could never be the case with language precisely because textual language is a product of consciousness. One cannot just "feel up" a language; a language must be "thought up."

To consciously create a literature expressive of a Black aesthetic, we necessarily must first think up what we mean by a Black aesthetic. Dr. Cheikh Anta Diop's *The Cultural Unity of Black Africa* was as important to me in my "thinking up" process (i.e., codifying a Black aesthetic), as was the political theory of Amílcar Cabral in helping me recognize and define the revolutionary character of people-based cultural work.

Particularly applicable was Diop's critique of tragedy and his advocacy of African optimism. Diop located the seeds of the tragic view of life in acceptance of the concept of "original sin."

> The themes [of tragedy] always deal, through the action of destiny, with a blind fatality which tends systematically to destroy a whole race or line of descent. They all betray a feeling of guilt, original with and at the same time typical of the Northern cradle. Whether it is a question of Oedipus or the Atrides and Agamemnon, there is always a flow, a crime committed by the ancestors, which has to be expiated irremediably by their descendants, who, from this fact and despite whatever they do, are utterly condemned by fate. Aeschylus tried to reduce the severity of this state of affairs by doing his utmost to introduce the idea of justice, which would allow an innocent posterity no longer to be punished, but to be absolved.
>
> The Semitic conception is identical. The original sin was committed by the very ancestors of the human race and all humanity, condemned from this time to obtain its bread by the sweat of its brow, had to atone for it. This point of view has been adopted and taught by modern religions such as Christianity and Islam.

The importance to me of Diop was that without the mystification of Yacub (the mad scientist who supposedly created "White people") or any other resort to racialism to explain human activity, he offered both an interpretation of the Eurocentric worldview and a human-centered explanation of a sub-Saharan African worldview. Regardless of whatever dreams and aspirations I or any of my peers hold, without rigorously researched, intellectual conceptualizations we would always end up proposing a mystical conceptualization of a Black aesthetic—mystical in the sense that one is asked to simply accept "Blackness" based on a belief system rather than on an interpretation of material reality. Such mysticism is another face of the biological fallacy mentioned earlier on.

Worldwide travel has disabused me of the notion of Black exceptionalism, e.g. "it's a Black thing; you wouldn't understand." Just as, to paraphrase Terence, there is nothing human that is foreign to me, certainly I as a human being need neither be perceived nor projected as foreign to any other human being. My chosen task as a writer is to locate the Black experience within the continuum of human experience. If I could understand the world, then certainly the world could understand me.

Diop gave me insight not only into myself but into the world at large, as well as insight into my relationship to others in the world. I am profoundly influenced by his conceptions of African culture. *I Enter Your Church* is Diopian in its concepts of relationships.

Hofu had been my first conscious attempt to do this. I intuitively stepped off into areas about which I had limited concrete understanding. From the beginning, I had felt the direction I wanted to go, and I had moved with that sensually perceived spirit in my heart. But now there is more than just a song in my heart; there is also something in my head.

For example, in ordering the poems in *Church*, I decided to utilize a structure of birth, maturity, death and rebirth. After I had completed and assembled the manuscript, I read a reference to this same philosophical system in *Signs and Symbols: African Images in African-American Quilts* by Maude Southwell Wahlman. The author pointed out that the diagrams on some of the quilts were replications of African cosmographs. She went on to point specifically to a Kongo cosmograph built on the same four-part philosophy that I'd thought was my thought.

As soon as I read it, I was happy. I prefer to be aboriginal in my modernity rather than novel (or what some call "original"). In essence, the preexistence of this African cosmology meant in part that I had intellectually aligned myself with my ancestral foundation. This was cause for great rejoicing.

For my part I had arrived at this place, as many artists do, via an intuitive leap. I had no specific concrete knowledge in hand, but I had cultural predispositions and subtextual teachings, which were the result of years of study—so it can also be argued that *Church*'s structure was simply a qualitative transformation of the quantitative mass of information I had consumed. Unavoidably there was a buildup of theories and experiential reflections posited by a wide variety of writings and conversations. For me all of this reached a critical mass in the beginning years of the nineties.

Regardless of whether coincidental or logical (albeit subconscious), this structure illustrated the basic unity of African culture. The closer we get to our total selves (i.e. the selves we were, are, and will to be/come), the more likely will be our convergence with both ancient and futuristic Afro-centered concepts.

Because I focus on culture, I believe that Africa is not simply land; Africa is people. In fact, not only are African Americans (all over the Diaspora) examples of African people, but the culture we produce is African culture even as it is also the product of accretions. In the final analysis, our people in general are always more important than any specific piece of land. I do not mean to imply that the continent of Africa is of negligible concern, but simply that it is not an abstract concern in and of itself—and it is a concern that can only be appreciated in concert with a concern for African people worldwide.

Some believe, as the Bible says, there is nothing new under the sun. In philosophical essence that may be true, but in fact, as Great Black Music demonstrates, out of Africa (the people), always something new. Africa is both the history and the future of my poetry.

Give thanx.

coda: in order for something to come out, you got to put something in

haiku #125

drum between my legs,
my horn blowing into the
dawn, dance with me please

A Black Aesthetic: Where I'm Coming From/Going To

1. Affirm life.

No art is completed until it is connected to the people (at the very least another person). Everything of value I have ever experienced has been consummated in a social setting (even if the society was the elemental couple procreating/enjoying life), and this is particularly true of art.

Every expression requires a transmitter, a message and a receiver—and, of course, whatever it takes to make all three work. In the West, the artist is severed from the audience (or the "auditors" as Julio Finn says). My art is incomplete without an audience because our culture is a culture of affirmation.

The old folks used to say, when you enter a room, speak to the people who are already there. When we enter the room of Black culture we should speak to the ancestors and we should expect to get a reply—after all, the ancients are culture(d) and will surely respond when spoken to.

Affirmation leads us to appreciate the continuum of life. Louis Armstrong would never have been whole, not to mention noble and bold, without the ancestors (King Oliver and Buddy Bolden) in his horn even when he blew notes that had never been blown before. By creating something new from something old, Louis, and Langston Hughes too, became ancestors of the future. These are the people we go back to in order to know who we are in the present. To be mature is to make yourself worthy of being an ancestor.

2. Make a joyful noise.
Step up and sing. Dance and music are the two most basic gestures of the soul. Yes, work is necessary for physical survival, but art is necessary for soul's survival. Dance because it is the movement of our bodies, our physical selves consonant with the grace and fluidity of life motions stylized in recognition of and emulation of the beauty and the power of the cosmos, the creator. Music because that is how we create imaginary worlds, how we enrich our imaginations, and it is our enriched imaginations that enable us to figure out how to withstand the mundanity of day to day slavery.

Dance, properly done, of course, is about being earth like. Duke Ellington and Sun Ra were always playing for dancers because until you move like the earth circling the sun, like rings around Saturn, like the breezes shaking the leaves, like the motion of the ocean, until you move you do not understand that the basic throb of life is Eros. Stillness is death. At the core of every dance is the celebration of the physical which necessarily leads to arousal. All of our dances, to a greater or lesser extent, are erotic because they celebrate life. There is nothing more human, more basic than dance. Nothing.

I approach my poetry as song precisely because song is the synchronizing of the soul with the body. Black song is, or ought to be, the sound of the body moving through life, the sound of the body being beaten or being loved. Song is a cry—just what a baby does. Song expresses our feelings, anxieties, desires and longings, our aspirations and our despairs, both hope and resignation. What is strongest about our songs is the quality of our expressive emoting, declarations unmediated (and hence, uncensored) by the workings of the mind. The mind unavoidably is circumscribed by the rules and regulations, taboos and qualifiers, of whatever society or civilization one finds oneself in.

If you only (or even, mainly) think about what you are singing, think about the music you are making, then you are not sharing your truest feelings, emotions. You are not sharing your total self. You are legislating your life, being a politician. There will necessarily be a discontinuity between what you say you are about and what you feel and desire. This discontinuity inevitably leads to guilt, anxiety and/or rage (especially when we realize that the expression of some (many?) of our deepest emotions is restricted, if not prohibited, by this society).

The purpose of the noise, the joyful noise, in my art is to disrupt the status quo and free the captive emotions.

The reason our music and dance are about freedom is because they are uncivilized. Uncivilized in the sense of unregulated by the social and moral authorities of America. The profoundness of our song and dance is that expressive participation in the making of music reinforces our resolve to be free. After the music, we are emboldened and are ready to take on the police—whether by actually dancing in the street or simply rejecting bourgeois propriety. I believe that if I can write a poem that helps people feel what freedom feels like, then, experiencing it momentarily within the ritual of art, they will desire it in their daily lives and hence will, of their own accord, think of ways to free themselves from the restrictions of this society.

3. Pro(Re)claim the blues.

The blues is a musical response to the socially restrictive, psychologically suppressive, and physically oppressive life we endure in America. The essence of the blues is primal, elemental rather than elaborate (i.e. intellectually deep). The blues is the elegance of emotional survival stripped of any social pretensions or prohibitions—which is why the thematic range may appear limited to those looking for intellectual stimulation. But far from being a limitation, the blues' raw power is what has preserved us.

The blues did more than artistically describe or replicate the essence of life. Being the ritual music that it is, the blues actually inspired and activated two essential qualities: facing up to the brutalness of life and seeking the community of love.

The reason the blues makes us happy even as it moans about pain is because it is mentally healthy to face the facts of life, the painful, the "evils," the wrongs, the losts. Facing adversity rather than suppressing our rage, our anger, our shame, our inadequacies, whatever. Indeed, that is why there seems to be so much violence in the blues, people singing about killing a lover, murdering with a knife, poison, hands, hammer or a gun. Those lyrics are expressions of real impulses and desires, the real rage that one feels when one is wronged. Rather than sublimate those seeming base emotions, the blues singer shouts them out in a cathartic voice that releases the individual from the need to express the desire through actual mayhem.

Do not misunderstand, the blues is not therapy because therapy implies illness. The blues is the ounce of cathartic prevention that is better than the pound of psychiatric cure. The healthy personality/society seeks to prevent mental illness, rather than solely treating it.

Facing up is healthy. And it feels good to publicly acknowledge these facts of life. Polite society would have us suppress feelings, but when we suppress our real feelings where does the pain go? If we push rage down deep into the personality and deny it an outlet, sooner or later it will manifest itself in one way or another. This is why civilization is neurotic, particularly American life with its myriad denials of reality. After all is said and done, what is civilization but a seasoning process that makes a slave "polite and obliging"?

Those who consider the blues profane are reacting to what they consider an affront to their aspirations toward the norms of a society that has enslaved them. Resultantly, and not unsurprisingly in this context, the more Blacks become like the Whites they aspire to be, then the more those same Blacks oppress and/or exploit their own Black selves. We Blacks become collaborating agents and maintainers of our own oppression. This oppression also assumes an intellectual dimension manifested in our disdain for the earthy, the funky, the "primitive," all of which is precisely what the blues is.

In this context, I have come to believe that my task as a poet is to confront the unmentioned, the avoided, the suppressed. My task is to emotionally confront rather than to intellectualize. In this connection, poetry is most persuasive in that it is built on a foundation of emotion rather than intellect, cathartic rather than therapeutic. Poetry is the linguistic expression of emotions. This is the structure that the blues gives to my work.

By extension, jazz is blues-based expression expanded by intellectual perceptions. In one of my poems I describe jazz thusly:

> you got to blues i believe, you Black, you
>   got to blues,
> or gospel, or rhythm & blues, or jazz, yes
>   jazz, jazz,
> now that's just another kind of blues with a
>   mind of its own,
> intelligent blues, thinking about things
>   blues, want to know
> blues, want to be blues, new day, sunrise,
>   yes, sunrise of
> that sun gonna shine when the morning
>   come day blues, but
> jazz is still blues, you can tell all them great
>   jazz players,
> they is blues, each and everyone of them,
>   blues masters,
> think of one, anyone, if they can't blues,
>   they can't jazz...

Blues and jazz, gospel (actually the whole of Baptist liturgy), folk music forms—Black music as a whole is the basic underpinning of my poetry. Even when I use the haiku structure, I do so consistent with the aesthetic demands of Great Black Music.

4. Seek unity with all.
We are citizens of the world. We belong to the cosmos. We must stop viewing the world strictly in racial terms, i.e. as White, Black and Foreign. We must understand that just as we socially belong to the world culture of humankind, in a very primordial physical sense we literally belong to and are inextricably part and parcel of the earth. In a psychic sense our souls belong to a larger cosmic scene: the great energy field of life. This is the necessary metaphysical component of our mundane expressions, the eternal analog to our temporal existence here on earth. Religion in general is simply (or complexly) an attempt to articulate this most profound connection.

I used the concept of energy field for specific reasons: all of life is relative, neither created nor destroyed only transformed, and depending on where we are on the continuum at the moment, it is manifested in a physical form. But even when we are physical, within our physical bodies the life energy force cries out for reunion with the cosmos, thus our desire to become one with god (the life force).

As I worked out this ideology, I struggled to insert those discoveries into my work. The poem "Earth Day" is a good example.

Earth Day

daily, once we arrive
we should ask ourselves what are we doing
to make the earth glad
that we are here

walking its face
breathing and being

does our living
help or hurt other
life forms

every time we celebrate
a birthday we should use the
occasion to reaffirm our pledge

to make the earth
glad that we are here

So, at base—writing the word "so" at this point requires another aside. Here is Zora Neal Hurston's explanation for my linguistic use of "so":

> In story telling "so" is universally the connective. It is used even as an introductory word, at the very beginning of a story. In religious expression "and" is used. The trend in stories is to state conclusions; in religion, to enumerate.

So, at base, the blues (and by extension all the other forms of Great Black Music) signifies the structure onto which I affix my specific remembrances and life experiences, as well as my intellectual speculations and conclusions. That is how I write my poetry.

* * *

You got to dream before you can analyze the meaning, and you've got to create a body of work before you can codify a poetic code. Thirty years is a long time. Only after you've gotten to the tail can you tell what the whole looks like.

I did not consciously start out trying to define an aesthetic. For that matter, I was not even guided by an aesthetic, i.e., a codification of beauty. I started moving strictly on a feeling, not a thought. I wanted to sing, and I had to figure out how. Even though I didn't know what I was doing, I didn't hesitate to move forward with the verve and arrogance characteristic of youth.

To this day, I don't know why I became a word singer. Carrying and concretizing the spirit was something I had to do, came crying into this world to do. Like breathing, I could not avoid creative expression. I was born to sing and knew it when I first heard the blues. My whole soul shook, something like when you climax but with more passion and with more lasting effect.

But here I am. This is my story; this is my song. Reflecting on how I got over is how I developed my theory of climbing. I didn't learn this in school; it wasn't written in a book. I'm not sure my elevator will lift you up, but I've shared all the secrets I know.

A special shout out to my son, Mtume ya Salaam, who was the line editor for this manuscript. Once I decided to focus exclusively on myself as a poet, as I wrote the text, Mtume suggested cuts, questioned items to include, edited for both flow and comprehension, and served as an excellent sounding board for the overall development, as well as for some of the particular philosophical points. The effort to combine both autobiography and aesthetic theory would have been much less effective were it not for Mtume's valuable insights and editing skills.

Like we always used to sign off: If there is something of value here, take it and pass it on, the rest leave alone.

Everything's gonna be alright.

If somebody asks you
Who sang this song.
Tell them Kalamu ya Salaam,
Been here and gone.

July 1994

POETRY

from *THE BLUES MERCHANT*, 1969

STATE/MEANT

BLKARTS WRITING (OR WHAT I'M

TRYING TO GET IN - TO

MEANS MAINLY TO SHARE

EXPERIENCES, FEELINGS, THOUGHTS, IDEAS

& SUCH, TO COMMUNICATE

LOVE OF PEOPLE (PEOPLE-BLACKS)

WHITES TAKEN COLLECTIVELY ARE NOT PEO

BLKS TAKEN INDIVIDUALLY USUALLY

END UP EMULATING COLLECTIVE WHITES

I MEAN ONLY TO SAY

HOW I AM BUT I AM

NOT ME BUT I AM WE

THE WE WHO ARE FIGHTING TOGETHER

FOR OUR LIBERATION

I SHALL NAME MY FIRST CHILD

SALAAM, CARRY A GUN

BE BLK & ONE DAY DIE

PEACE&LIBERATION

from *PAMOJA TUTASHINDA*, 1973

give a speech/talkin abt 'da problem'

I.
give a speech to reach
the masses
the common
man, brotherdude and sisterlady
    walkin on the sidewalk past trash, and no
    love at all and the disorder of weird
    blue dressed sadists & stores with dummies buying and
        selling
    cheap cloth in the window
    and, of course, the dude that didn't
    just didn't return even after
    promising just the other night he would,
    he might, and the eternal, eternal baby whines
    spilling long off into the night becoming morning
    and the mourning, the moaning and work
    and a male supervisor who knows you but doesn't really
    know you and who maybe hates you and at the veryleast
    could care less about you and how you feel this moment
    and who makes much more money than you for doing much
        less
    work than you do and the too high cost of car notes plus
    insurance and weekly, daily gas
    for that car and monthly notes always coming too soon
    on most everything else
give a speech to reach
the masses, to reach this, to reach us
who are tired of words?
give a speech

II.
past this jack but haven't we heard this talk umpteen times befo
how many poems have you heard in the last two years

our bodies can't digest paper and books and even if we could
could we afford to buy enough of them, our international bodies
that can speak every language the European can, our bodies
past this, our bodies
some bodies we are randomly floating which ever
way the gravity of alien situations attract us
some heavy bodies flashing through space
pulled by everybody else, dragged, tied to everybody else,
our bodies are somebodies though in a highly, highly
    underdeveloped stage
some bodies desperately in need of identity, purpose and direction
somebodies, some bodies are sayin
that's the problem nah
niggers talk too much
but is it? is that
really the problem now
    is talk why our life expectancy is so short
    is talk why we eat so badly
    is talk why we work a week for one day's wages
    is talk why everybody laughs at us on television
    is talk why we spend so much time in jail
    is talk why we have no money, no power, no land
    is talk why all our schools are dumb, our teachers dumber
    is talk why nobody likes us
    nobody like the negro
    is talk the cause of that
    are we here because of talk
    think about that,
    did talk rape your grandmomma, red?
    did talk make you eat pork, abdul?
    did talk cut off the gas&lights last night, rhetta?
    did talk to this or was it organized people
        taking advantage of our ignorance
        or was it organizations
        moving while we slow

motion over the shells
looking for the pea that was ate long ago?
not talk but organization
not speech but speed and power
and politics
politics bringing down some control
of our social actions and values
that is what put us here
and thas what keeps us here
that and our continued ignorance of how
how our enemies operate
how they operate on us
how they keep us afrikans being everything but afrikans
how they keep us working for the good of everybody
else but us, ourselves
how they keep us fighting against ourselves seldom even
shadow boxing
the beasts who feed on us, the usurers who make money
on us, the
blanks who live only through us and, even, the
simple average American square
whose comfort is thanks to us
they keep us like pets and house plants
knowing, knowing that america's best friend is
"the negro"

III.
do we want out of this
out of this disease, no ease, not rest, only trouble and turbulence
and
lives almost too hard to live with grace
out of this filth and sad times, poverty and the jaded
stale breath of Nixon breathing on our lives
we want away from wpa built and state inspired projects and
their educational adjuncts

vulgar public classrooms where the teachers make us stupid
we want a better life, don't we shirley, huh rufus, huh danny,
am i telling the truth rose, don't we want to rise, huh?

then organize
organize to control
control the space we occupy,
control all that space as best we can
the first space being of course, the body, the flesh and
muscle, brain and mind body, control that from hair tip
to toenail, discipline it, i.e., self-control it
exercise power over it, i.e., self-determine it,
    self-defend it, self-respect it
work it out, get it up early in the morning and run it, exercise
it, take it out the bed at six, seven at the latest, move with
the wind with it, beat back sloth with it, beat back laziness
and inefficiency with it, feed it honey and powerful food
less grease & grit, more juice and fruit
like we don't do now, yes, do that to our bodies in order
to control that space we occupy
to control that space we occupy
organize, organize first yrself, the person you
meet in the morning mirror, the self that is so tired
really so tired of being black and beautiful and yet incased in
    this ugly land,
how can we be really black and beautiful and be in this ugly land,
look around it, smell it, taste it, touch it, the streets and sidewalks
full of garbage and days old dogshit, the water full of small
floating flakes and smelly chemicals, the air thick anough to whip,
look around it, cars stacked up on the highways pppphhhh,
vvoooommmmmmmmn, psshhoooooottttt, putputputt, poop,
    farting, i.e.,
passing gas on us, how can we be really beautiful
unless we organize and clean up
clean up first self, wash everyday, change clothes and lifestyles

in favor of the better, the realer, the truer to what we are
we must clean up
leave off smoking everything but the air outside
stop living in dirt, make our houses vessels of clean which is beauty
stop the senseless curses, make our mouths vehicles of clean
    which is beauty
we must clean up self first and alter the image we have from X
rated movies that show us death, decadence and degeneracy
we must clean up
we must first clean up self
and organize
organize self to work
organize self to study
organize self to give of everything we have
to share everything we have, to share everything we have, to
    share
    everything
    we have

IV.
organize
organize negroes, booker
organize blacks, marcus
organize afros, mary
organize niggers, brother & sister
organize, i.e. get um together, put it in order
listen now we gon need a plan and some land
    we gon need some space, i.e., vital and strategic living room
        to grow on
    we gon need some thought, i.e., an ideology, a system of
        beliefs
    we gon need some resources, i.e., some food, shelter, clothing
        and raw materials
we gon need some communications i.e., some exchanging of
    ideas and information

we gon need some order, i.e., some putting things in their place,
    in their proper priority
organize
how we gon organize the negro
who, by the way, is us
the black
who is us
the afro
who is us
the nigger
who is, whether we hip to it or not, still us
    we gon need some love, i.e. some working together
        in unity
how we gon organize
    we gon need some values, i.e. a reference other
        than
    how i feel this morning, or what the leader said do
    or the latest European fad, we need values, a
        reference from which
    to come from, to go forward with, to aim toward,
        an afrikan framework
    that will make all our lives precise and predictable
        and finally good
    and better than we are now without a ruler to
        measure
how we gon do that
how can we all do that
easy, step by step, one by one starting with self
and tiny, tiny crawls that barely flex our leg muscles, which must
    be soon running
easy but always long, hard and continuously, i.e., continuously
    aaa-heee
    start with the easy, give a dime a day
    start with the easy, run one block a day
    start with the easy, read for five minutes a day

start with the easy, eat one fruit a day
start with the easy, volunteer fifteen minutes a day
start with the easy and organize to do the
undifficult
don't worry about the heavy problems
all the heavy problems ain't goin nowhere
just develop self step by step and one by one
we'll get to everything in due time
come on now, long uh, un huh, hard uh, un huh, and
continuously aaa-heee
go on get um roberta kill the enemy softly
come on jesse push the crackers off our space
do it wilt court yr sisters
whip it up all let's stay together
actualize it maulana really get "US" together
keep growing haki teach on the planet
spiritualize it imamu raise our congress
just be naturally for real people and we gon make it
just be all that we can be people and we gon make it
gon make it better—black un huh, i.e., with color,
culture and consciousness
gon make it easier—afrikan unnn huh, i.e., with
pan afrikanism, revolutionary
nationalism and ujamaa
gon make it, gotta, got ta make it
workin together, in love, sunshine, in and out,
pain and rain
sweet bless, lord, ancestors, ancients, oldtimers dig
our species
singing swinging and balling through space
kazi pamoja tutashinda
together, organized as a world body
which we are
a world body, afrikans are a world body, we are all
over the world

only now at this time just not fully organized, not
together but
gon get it together, gon get it all together jammed
up there
like jigsaw puzzle pieces pulled apart waiting for
the patient
fingers of committed bloods to weave the various
threads of
our separated afrikan selves back into a single
multi-colored
dazzling fabric
bits and pieces right now are scattered everywhere
not by winds and chance but by slavery and imperialism
bits and pieces placed brazenly everywhere in need to be put
back together
again but not by magick or prayer but by hard work, by the
long strong hard kazi, kazi, kazi of
organized afrikans
organized afrikans, can you image it
organized afrikans, even better be it, for real, no dream but
actual
organized afrikans together, you me us WE
together and organized and, guess what, yep, you bet
together we will win
PAMJOA TUTASHINA!

from *REVOLUTIONARY LOVE*, 1978

RE TAIL & MERCHANDISE, ghetto time

growing up
old heads
school
young bloods

sweet things pass
constantly

it
stiffens
hard
wanting that
the sun frowns
a sip of beer
a swallow a wine

wet dreams in the
daytime

"see that,
young blood . . ."

eye trails thigh

he laughs

"FINDUM,
FOOLUM,
FUCKUM,
FOREGETUM!"
he laughs

a boy is born

a black man
dies

from *OUR WOMEN KEEP OUR SKIES FROM FALLING*, 1980

OUR WOMEN KEEP OUR SKIES FROM FALLING

our women keep our
skies from falling
our days from dying
our nights from crying

carrying deep
within themselves
the sacred sun loves
of African-american lives

embers which fire
black generations are
securely embedded betwixt
broad baobabian hips
and gleam sparkling forth
from deep lakes of
blue/black brown
dark ebony eyes

their song is
healing song, and
calling song, and
culture song, and
though no one can
stop the rain

our women keep our
skies from falling

from *A NATION OF POETS*, 1989

MY STORY, MY SONG

this is my story
my song, i will sing these blues,
tho they stole my tongue

this is my story, the story of slavery is their story
the story of survival is my story, the lacerations aching
my back were meant to break me down into subhuman
submission
but the balm of my music salved my suffering
and when the whiplash fever broke, in the morning i rose
and went once again to meet the man, we all rose
every black one of us still alive
and went to meet that man

the same man who had erased our blackboard, crashed our
computer heads,
burned our books and cooked our elders in superstitions and
trivial
remembrances slave traders called fairytales from when massa
was animals,
animal-like, wolves and bats, this same man who reduced
religion
to drinking blood, eating flesh and birthing without fucking,
who
tried to make nakedness an obscenity, work a cruelty, dance a sin
and beauty strange pictures of pale women and bald-head babies,
they pissed in the same water they drank, ate alone, made
enemies of everyone, and said that they would save us from
eternal
damnation, but worse of all they erased my blackboard so i don't
even
know who i am, i know i am not them, but who as i

what do i remember before being born again, spit from the
moving womb
of wood that carried me cross water for nineteen days or more, i
do not
know the words of my history, i can not recall
two generations back anymore, i can't remember who i was
before
i became who i am, nevertheless, even tho
i am unlettered, i am not illiterate
i know my history happened and so i sing my song,
the can't remember but will not forget song, i moan
the soul hole nothing foreign can fill, i hum
faintly recalled melodies and fuse them into guitared
praisepoems,
from what's here at hand i fashion as best i can an approximation
of what i had and what i dare dream is to come,
even though i don't remember my past, even though
the master stole my tongue, slit it and threw it into the sea,
nothing can still me cause still i sing, even though
it's illegal for me to call out even the words
of my history, still, i sing

so when massa asked with smug contempt: where
were our books, i just moaned, um-hummmm-hummmmm
having only books and no blues, he can't understand,
having only a to z he can't follow no long snake moan
what takes red disaster, colors it blue and miraculously turns
white reality into black survival, he ain't
got no books what could do that, he don't
have no key to the kingdom of humanity, no blues,
no "mama, mama, mama, i will always call your name,"
sung to the shadow of a lover gone away, "wit out you mama,
nuthin ain't the same," no flat foot good rockin tonight til dawn,
no cake walk born of cotton sack shuffle, no music to take a
whip

and make a smile, when i stroke this heah guitar string and sing
"baby, baby, baby, bossman, he don't know my mind, he see me
laughin'
but i'm laughin' to keep from cryin', a-oohhhh loooorrrd,
lawdy, lawdy, lawdy do, what i don't with him,
i wants to do with you, ohhhhh," i'm talking bout the blues,
where are your books he said,
where is your constitution, niggra
but he dance stiff, in a square, and paints his house white
wears hats but no masks, dons seven layers of clothes in the sun
with a silk rope choking his neck, telling a slave about america's
great
bill of rights, where are your great documents the thief says
knowing he done sacked timbuctu, stole half of egypt, and
wrecked
every kingdom he could find, where are your words
and all i could say was um, um, um
meet me at the crossroads round quarter past midnight
bring yo fiddle, yo harp or drum, get ready to beat the devil
and shout blues til morning come,
where are your explorers he wanted to know
stroking the guitar i hope to always hear
where are your merchants and businessmen
i say here the lady come, market woman strutting,
basket on her head, all our blackness been the blues,
it's been the blues that brought us on thus far
and the blues gon take us home, i sing my song

the blues, what else but that wail
could capture the wound of being torn from mama/africa's
green, green/blue, blue/brown, brown/red, red/black breast
i hungered for those bountiful breasts now called jungle
and them i could not remember any specifics
and then i forgot even the generalities
but still there was a sadness stuck in me mouth

that made me wanna suck on something i had not tasted
for so long, bye and bye i am most shame
to admit, i could not recall the contours, the surging swell
of that bronze nipple, nor the rise and dimpled darknesss
surrounding, that areola of sweetness, you can not know
what it means not to be able to remember your mama's breast,
but the blues remembers what i do not remember
so without even being able to explain it, i feel this song
surging inside of me grinning and shouting and i feed
this song my every question, my why for, my how come
my what did i do to be so black and blue
and it answers me bye and bye, when the morning come
the morning, the dawning, the new day, not the same old
same old, not the moaning for my baby, baying in the moonlight,
not the train whistle out of here that takes us to another here,
no train can cross the water, not the voting blues, the politician
blues, the welfare blues, the public school blues, but when
the morning come, it's been the blues that fed my human hunger
for release, it's the blues what kept me company
walkin' down these mean streets, it's been the blues
that loved me when nobody would call my name
it's been the blues that hugged me when i thought i was gone
    insane
this music been my maker when my master was so mean to me
been my sweet salvation when nothing good i could see
what else but that wail, could carry me cross yonder field
the blues is what has saved me, the blues is the only real

black is the basic color of the blues
not black like shackled nights, or cotton rows
at plantin' time stretching far as the eye can see,
no, not even the black of the bruise the lynch rope leaves
not just that black, but the basic people black of us,
the mandingo, fulani, ashanti, ibo, the all of us
whatever we were, never mind whatever they tried to make

us be, no matter, our humanity sang survival,
we were black we became blue, our blackness begat
the blues and the blues bespoke our blackness

but all our blues don't have to be blues, yaknow,
gospel is blues, just sung in a choir with different words
and calvinist chords churcified, flattened and fitted with flyin'
rhythms on which you climb and ride up side king jesus golden
    chariot
and seek salvation over on the other side, make you think you
done died, cept the blues blues always withstood the pain
of living black, never forgot it, never ignored it, never
made believed that pain did not exist, never promised nothing
but survival, i know some of us like to dream of heaven, like to
look forward to dyin' and livin' again and never dying again,
but really gospel ain't nothin' but another kind of blues,
just mostly the wishin'&hopin' side, not the slide and moan,
and never the jelly, nor the big brass bed
do they make love in heaven, it would take a blues man
to ask that question, but the gospel is blues too, i reckon,
well sort of leastways, any song what can make a slave strong,
strong enough to stand slavery's reign got to have some blues in it,
and then rhythm and blues ain't nothin' buy havin' a good time
dancing mostly, a music for peoples to party by, like up to the
    jukejoint
when we would throwdown and shake what for, shake um on
    down
lil red light, lil blue light, ahhh yesss, but it's hard to sell
a million tears, but we needed the blues, the blues is
what makes us feel alive when whiteness keeps tryin'
to grind us down, the blues is our birth certificate
the description of how we was born

if you don't mind not knowing what dust god molded you from
than you can go head on and not know the blues, but me myself,

i carries my past deep inside my dream pocket,
knows it like i knows my teeth, how can i ignore what's me
you got to blues i believe, you black, you got to blues,
or gospel, or rhythm & blues, or jazz, yes jazz, jazz,
now that's just another kind of blues with a mind of its own,
intelligent blues, thinking bout things blues, want to know
blues, want to be blues, new day, sunrise, yes, sunrise of
that sun gonna shine when the morning come day blues, but
jazz is still blues, you can tell all them great jazz players,
they is blues, each and everyone of them, blues masters,
think of one, anyone, if they can't blues, they can't jazz,
still, nowadays so many of us have forgotten or refuse to
    remember
the blues, our blues bag is neigh bout empty, we don't
carry that sack no mo, so where will our words come from
if we don't have the blues, what will we say, what will we
remember, what can we possibly be, if we don't have the blues?
maybe today's slavery has become too easy,
perhaps someone has sutured our birth wound, healed us
of that longing to know who and what we were,
what the klan couldn't kill look like we gon let die
for lack of love, look like now we don't much listen to us selves,
mr. can't sing blues black man be tellin' me the blues is bout
submission, shuffling and stuff too ugly to hang on yonder wall,
but submission is silence and silence is not my song

i know everything must change
but still and all, all goodbyes ain't gone
just cause we don't dance like we used to
don't mean we got to give up our song
the blues is our literature, our rights, our wrongs
we done both suffered and survived, survived and sung
not just waded through the slaughter but come out
whistlin' "the orange sun is shinning, the wide sky is blue
i'm offering you my sweet and tender love baby,

honey fresh as morning dew, i'm a rusty-dusty black man, mama
just a singing a song to you, i'm a oak tree strong louisiana man
askin' you, woman, mama, what cha gonna do?"

where are your books he asked me
as he mutilated and stole my tongue
not expecting any answer to hear
but i survive his sufferation
and answer with a glorious sound
as i gave the world my song

from *WHAT IS LIFE?*, 1994

sometimes i think i have not done enough to make the world safe for love

(a letter to Linda/i waz just thinking)

safe for dreams, safe for children, for unfenced flower
gardens and for lonely late night walks just because
at two a.m. on any given night you want to walk and
think, and think and walk, alone, down some street, near or
far from home, and safe for visa-unnecessary visits from world
lovers and comrades, from dignitaries and unknowns from
nations whose names we can't spell, safe for teen-agers
to have slumber parties unchaperoned and sleep seven
on the floor with the front door forgotten
unlocked, for medical care always available
for a baby coughing at midnight almost choking
and unable to sleep and parents unable to sleep
and no money necessary to get this child treated, for
world cinema shown at the corner show, for 24-hour jazz
radio and reggae radio, and opera and blues day
blues night, for celebratory tangos and drum choirs from
ghana and television shows of poets reading, safe for
committed literature uncensored, printed in popular
editions and sold for a quarter or so at the
local newsstand, every local newsstand, in every
country, in every language that's readable,
literature as abundant as guns and bombs are today, like
that, right next to fruit and vegetables, on top
of the counters of corner stalls, safe for
not having to flinch when a police siren screams
or even when three or more policemen come walking toward
me, safe for an end to world leaders whose average age,
    temperament
and physical condition makes it impossible for them to dance
or giggle, for an end to bad drinking water and unending

nuclear waste, the threat of misinformation shrouded covert
operations, for the immediate cessation of the strategic blowing
of natural resources into space while urban-scapes
rot and become the dumping grounds for tons of non
biodegradable trash, safe for honoring human being with deeds
rather than cement statues with swords, rifles and flags
unpraised, for memorializing strugglers who have made a
    positive
difference by erecting libraries and cultural centers, hospitals
and bus stations named for them, safe for writing
to overseas friends and the postage rate lowered
for personal letters & picture post cards & cassettes,
safe for big black multi-ton whales to warble sub water and frolic
sticking their tails out of the sea as they dive up and down,
safe for the mental health of everyone and the housing
of the man who smells (his skin patina so weathered you can
not tell if he is black or white) sleeping on the steps of
some towering stone building in six layers of oversized
clothes dirty as the metropolitan sidewalk his head resting
in pigeon shit, for an end to looking at each other crooked,
influenced by some foolishness, we don't know where
it comes from, me sitting in my skin castle with racial
rooms that have one little window and a locked door, sitting
behind thick, class-erected walls breathing state air, squatting
in my gender fortress, and you just as vigilant holed-up
in yours, several moats of bad feelings and misunderstandings
separating us, safe for talking eye to eye instead of
communicating with hastily scribbled messages tied
to rocks that we bizarrely heave between us-selves,
back and forth, under the misleading title of official
government communiques, safe for an unconditional &
    immutable
world law which prohibits soldiers leaving the places
wherever they were born, for a 365-day-a-year amusement
park where we can send old war lords, ex-presidents, premieres

& prime ministers and all others who think they are qualified
to run, rule and ruin the world so they can play
games to their hearts' content and not hurt themselves nor
us, safe for smiles and honestly talking to people we've never
met before, for riding a bus home after midnight without
a gun, safe even for snakes to cross a road without
somebody's self-righteous bootheel crushing their heads simply
because they're a different kind of animal,
safe for artistic expression and yes, safe and sometimes also,
    really
safe all the time also, for silly expressions, and gentle
laughter as well as safe too for those screamers
that make your side hurt when your friends mimic the way you
    bug
your eyes when you are angry or the way i rub my jaw when
i am embarrassed, and we be walking down the street some
    spring
day eating hot apple pie licking our fingers on the way to tutor
and play ball with some kids somewhere, or is it the Black
Women's International Photo Exhibit called "Soul Eyes" that we
are going to, sometimes i know i haven't done enough
to make the world safe for love—i promise to do better.

from *GHOSTS*, 1995

GHOSTS

i have the smile of my great-grandmother seeing the end of
slavery
& you have the hairline of an uncle/an aunt
who never pressed nor otherwise chemically altered their hair

only fools don't intimately know ghosts,
the dna of humanity, leaping like porpoises slick out of the sea
and back into our walks, our mannerisms, the way we giggle
when nervous, blush when aroused, or spit fire words
in sputtering ocher anger facing back the cannibalism of
capitalism

ghosts are
just spirits fluttering angel breaths thru our corpuscles
the wing hum of hummingbirds motivating us to sound
snatches of remembered songs, lyrics formerly unheard
in this lifetime, psychically transmuted across eras,
mali melodies maintained, aural treasures from our undying
befores

face east, young people, face east
imagine each line in your hand an ancestor
how well do you know the thoroughness of yesterday,
the arching influence of the previous century, the retrograde
of rationality, so slow compared to the velocity
of history smashing into the protons of personality

imagine, your voice is the texture of sun yat-sen singing
a freedom song, your social erectness the reincarnate posture
of sitting bull standing barefoot his clear eyes kissing dark earth,
imagine, your breath the aroma of emiliano zapata biting the
bullet
of revolution and spitting fire on the butts of robber barons

and dark-faced overseers who are the psychological sons
of simon legree in their twisted brutality towards their own
    people,
the defiance of your unsurrendering war stance could be ghana's
yaa asantewaa hurling up the west coast facing down british
    guns
confident that the religion of resistance will always outlive
the technology of repression, you could be the heroics of history,
a phantasmagoria of sacred strugglers vivifying the surge
of timeless protoplasm which careens through your veins
and gives substance to the willfulness of your animated
    engagement
with the omnivorous enemies of the planet earth
ghosts are
sacred illuminations coloring our stratagems and meditations,
they are the realization of sanity, the moment we truly
    understand
just how wicked the west actually is, the translucent
lights on the front porches of our spirits beckoning, guiding our
soft footsteps on the path, heading back homeward bound
dancing into the social circle of our collective selves

ghosts remind us
each individual is more than one, a communal hope chest
of ancient dreams actualized in the present

i believe in ghosts, i do
because i would be soulless matter otherwise
i would be some french rationalist trying to intellectually
    manufacture
& market the focus of life as the ego of thought, would be
some compassionless corporate ceo with spiritual arthritis
uninformed by the blessings of sharing, while pretending
that material possessions elevate morality as if you are what you
    own

rather than are what you do/be in relation to others and the
world

ghosts
do not like vaults and crypts, nor fences and forts
real ghosts prefer sensitive personalities and wild open spaces,
every time we inhale a leaf shakes,
a tree or a weed offers us breath
give thanks to the grass for our daily inhalations

i am not a mystic
but i know there are ghosts
in the fecund topsoil which progress
callously covers with concrete,
i understand the reality that dust and dirt are airborne bones
pulverized by time into tiny particles

a rose by any other name is still the collected essence
of our forebearers grown through the life cycle into a fragrant
state
of petal soft beauty on a bud whose shape is nature's re-creation
of the vaginal portal, whose redness is an honoring
of feminine life force and the blood value of matriarchy

if you do not believe in ghosts
where do you think your spirit will be
when the corporeal temple of your familiar
crumbles into seemingly insignificant pebbles of peat, or
when your temporal sanctuary dehydrates
once disconnected from the moisturizing of life's cosmic juice,
when the way station of your flesh altar no longer receives
offerings
& when you revert to what you were before your human being
was conceived and made flesh via the union of your parents,
won't you be a ghost then?

there are literally millions of lives in your little finger

the karma of colonialism will not be undone
not unless and until the ghosts that reside
in the hosts of color worldwide can find a culture
which resonates daily contentment,

there will be no end to the wandering search for the promised
land
unless and until ghosts can live
inside the wholeness of beating hearts synchronized
in embracement, respecting the healing touch
of every manifestation of life no matter how small, obscure,
or ostensibly insignificant,

no calming the tempest,
no mediation of the disruption of our heritage
not unless and until ghosts can emigrate
into a peace-filled community of souls such as we
ought to be, vessels of awareness, responsible in our openness
to offer wholesome residences for the motion flow
of history seeking future,
there will always be a wailing issuing out our mouths
unless and until ghosts can live and
comfortably reside, live, and rest inside, rest
in peace, rest in us

ghosts

peace

ghosts

rest

ghosts

in

ghosts

peace

ghosts

rest

ghosts

in

ghosts

us

IF YOU'RE STILL THE SAME AFTERWARDS IT WASN'T LOVE

(to nia, thanx for making me better)

to say
"i am touched

by you"

is to be
changed

/ into
a person neither of us
was before
entering the other

more open, a sun of sensitivity
emotionally nude, erupting joy
& willing to kiss life open mouthed
emoting the vibrancy of glow
endemic to souls in the flow

in fact, it's even unscientific
not to evol
ve/not to love, not to
grow & give back

the only humans who actually evolve
are lovers
all others
just simply fuck and reproduce
the transformation
of touch

that's all
love is

We Don't Stand A Chinaman's Chance Unless We Create A Revolution (*"There's A New World Coming"*)

To Fred Ho & Everyone In The World
Who Are Not Afraid Of The Future

Chance, like the lottery, is dependent on the universe
What the conditions of the competition are
How many of us competing and who's pullin' the numbers

Look at the world, my people, where we draw our borders
Determines who we are, defines our social status as a people

If we stop at the Atlantic & Pacific
We could just dumbly call all ourselves Americans
If we start at Canada
Then for certain we are deep in the South,
Down below the real Mason-Dixon line
If we start at Mexico & work our way north
Then most of us are just
Non-Spanish-
speaking, dark-skinned gringos

But if we go back into ourselves, into our souls
Our history and the reality of our befores
Then there is something greater than geography
That defines us

I am a political creature
Praxis, ideology put into practice
Defines a major part of me

I am also an individual particle of my people
My roots, blood and genealogy
Defines another part of me

But more than politics and biology combined
I am a human being, a creature defined
By the character and quality of my social
Relationships
Who I am, is very much
The way I relate to people, both my race & others

Is whether I lie about my realities
Or struggle to tell the truth

Is whether I want to get over by bullshiting
Or want to develop by facing & changing my reality

So what is a lie versus
What is the truth?

A lie is when we knowingly say the opposite of what
We are, were and strive to become
The truth is simply what is

Our problem is not just telling lies
But also being able to recognize lies
We've been lied to for so long

Believed lies for so long in the past that
Today we don't know the truth

How can we honestly know who we are
If we don't truthfully know who we were

Truth looks strange to us, sounds
Weird, even corny or square, is a foreign language
Certainly painful and discomforting, the truth is
A hard lesson to swallow when we've been
Filled up with lies, our bowels blocked by

Government cheese & our arteries hardened
By imbibing consumer prescribed drugs

You don't know it
But you don't really know anything
If all you know is what you have been
Taught in school combined with the limited
Education you get from media distortions of world
Realities

If you think dope in our lives is bad now,
That crack houses exemplify moral decay,
That we need to get back to the past
Then what do you think of opium dens
And native Americans besotted by alcohol

Chemical warfare
Is nothing new, especially in this nation of junkies
Where the twin drugs of tobacco & alcohol rule the roost

Consider this a gentle wake up call:

We don't stand a chinaman's chance
Of creating a better & more beautiful future
If we don't make a revolution

You don't stand a chinaman's chance
Is what people used to say to define hopelessness
You don't stand a chinaman's chance
Used to be a definition of a loser
But after Mao & crew did their do
A chinaman's chance got so good
That nobody played that number anymore

Regardless of the problems and perplexities
Of China's current state at least they got a chance,
A future & the whole world recognizes that

What about us, my people
Do we stand a chinaman's chance,
We, the underdogs in a horse race

The ice cubes trying to stand the heat of hell
The fifth wheel on a tricycle
Buying bus tickets to cross the ocean
Worshippers without a god
We who can't stand to reign
Will continue to suffer a million to one
Odds of redemption
Unless we create
A revolution

Plant the seed, raise the tree
Dig, we made America into a democracy

Now we must recreate this whole country
Into a multicultural community where all peoples
Can live & be their natural selves
Can live their traditions & carve out a future
Can call on their ancestors & give birth to healthy children
Can learn what they don't know & teach everything they do
Can honor the earth & respect the sacredness
Of all living beings

There will be no bright future for us
Unless we create & seize control of our lives
Consume no more than we produce &
Produce all we need to consume
Unless we define progress in terms

Of the quality of relationships &
Measure wealth by the status of the poor
No future until we consciously empower women &
Proudly display a healthy respect for diversity

No tomorrows unless we shut down
The hegemony of cave culture & reinstitute social circles,
Bring back the vision of the tepee, the hut &
Other architectural & social structures which avoid
The dominance of the box & straight line
Nothing will grow unless we merge
With the other rather than thinking separate is equal
We can only greet the dawn with smiles
By doing for self & sharing with all
By building marketplaces at the crossroads
Rather than forts on the frontiers
By learning the literature of the world
Rather than imposing a canon of monoculture

A true revolution
Motivated by the force of love
Sustained by the generosity of spirit
Is ultimately victorious not because it conquers
But rather because it endures
Outlasts exploitation & overcomes oppression

A revolution, a revolution
A revolution of the human
Body & soul, mind & consciousness,
A decisive change, after which
Nothing can ever be the same
Change is the external truth
Everything that exists becomes
Something other than what it now is

Some people think that ugly gon last forever
That whites will always rise to the top &
Revolution is impossible, i.e., that is the
Flat earth school of foolish thought

Those same people think
We don't stand a chinaman's chance
To create a revolution—you wanna bet

Whether through evolution or
Revolution, things have got to change

We, like all humans, will evolve or die
Regardless of what we think & do
We will either renew ourselves or
Become extinct

There is a new world coming
There will be a revolution
In our lifetime

The only question is where we gon be standing
What we gon be doing
Who we gon be loving
When it comes!

from *360°: A REVOLUTION OF BLACK POETS*, 1998

No Ordinary Waterfall

(for Gwen Brooks)

may your words: coiled concise, darkly bright, ever flow never
erode
nor recede but always be thought seed a growing green that feeds
the spirit thirst of us who sojourn in desert clime seeking
soil deep enough to support dense neo-african roots; gwen
love is you who blew syllabled breaths into politicized psyches,
exhaled stanzaed transmission which raised our imaginations
buoyed us with the simple leverage of speech booted on the black
rock of conscious lyrics sung precise as talk drum heartbeats
rhythmically sounded by skilled hands rapping life cycles
reverberating off the scarred hides of our time

you are no ordinary waterfall but a sacred pouring sparkling
liquid clear as crystal joy tears in grand motherly eyes
surveying with knowing surprise the accomplishments
of progeny who yesterday were but babbling babes;
gwen, we are the scribes, wordsmiths and versifiers
you inspired, our thymes succulent juice of precious fruit
grown ripe atop the griot height of mahogany poet trees
and watered by the elixired libation of our sagacious
queen mother humbly uttering a holistic incantation:
write as black as you be and be as black as all we
collected, resurrected, rightly rendered, remembered

snapshot: dawn in dar es salaam

our intimacy is as subtle as the mottled shade of shell colors
on a warm basket of cayenne scented boiled crabs
or, more likely, the faint hint of spearmint tea
silently seeping while your attention is turned
to spreading the beige soft of cashew butter across
the crisp of one slice of toasted sourdough
which innocently rests near the dark
of seeded unsugared strawberry jam freshly smeared
atop the face of the bread's twin—quiet contentment
is morning within our colorful kitchen where we are
as gaily nude as the golden gleam of early light
streaming through our window diagonally impressing
a translucent tattoo onto both the half sphere of your breast
& the upraised arm of my hand reaching to caress

from *WAYS OF LAUGHING*, 2009

Ways of Laughing

I look at the young women
in our class—Inola, my mother
is there in some of their eyes when they share
with each other whatever little they have: four pieces
of candy, two, or even three, are given away. On the lower back
of one is a tattoo, an adornment to beautify what is already
brown and beautiful, all of them wear colors
like the sky after a spring rain, moisture sparkling
in the atmosphere colored the most promising of colors, their
sharp voices are some times sweet, some times bitter
taking on the taste of their life experiences, their eyes
are so old to be housed in such youthful faces, despite
disasters they are still full of hope and the romanticism
of youth thinking that life is not uncaring, is not totally unfair, will
give them a chance to be something other than disappointed

like their earrings they come in all sizes and shapes, with different
ways of laughing

COSMIC DEPUTY, 1968-2019

A REPLY TO KELLY
(in post-katrina new o.)

after the rescue operation
never the same

the crisis had been bad and
the immediate recovery uncertain

the surgery to save
nearly killed

now get short of breath
just turning a corner
and seeing nothing
—literally nothing—
where my childhood once stood

ghosts walk the streets
not the peeps we ran into all the time
and embraced and laughed
our faces close in public
displays of affection

i was in city park recently
its greenery still beautiful proof
that no god cares
about punishing the affairs
of humans, instead sends us
both hurricanes & sunshine
thankfully more sunny days
than stormy days
and some days
i feel like a mouse in the corner
a greedy cat in the air descending

which is to say i'm sure
it's over

other days
i hear the bell and can evade
long before the asphyxiation of fear
fouls my hair and causes my nostrils
to flair in some vain attempt
to breathe

someone wrote and wanted to meet
me, i will send them
what anyone standing beside me
can see in my mirror
that image & as much of me
as is available that day to keep
the appointment

A Toast To You

like a new shoe
digs a shine

like a pencil
loves a sharp point

like a watch
lives to tell time

like a knee
must have a joint

i loves you

Aft/er

aft
er we've
(or should
i say
i'd)
made
love

i wanted to hold you, but you have bound up from our bed & are gone from my grasp well before i am sufficiently recomposed to open and clasp my arms, so i hold the thought of you

i have just shuddered, exploded myself, funneled liquid missiled into your moistness, am still gasping, only partially aware, sight is fuzzy, my thoughts are louder than anything in the air, i'll be all right in a moment

i hear you running the shower in the hall bath, the morning water covering your nakedness where moments earlier i joyfully was

outside the open windows a crow caws in the near distance, two streets away a dog desultorily barks, the wind moves a few leaves

our floors are terrazzo in some rooms, light colored carpet in others, overhead fans, enough wall space to hang art and photographs, rooms full of comfortable places to read
music floats from the small system, most of the time you punch up billie holiday, etta james singing billie holiday, nina simone mournful as billie holiday, or grover washington interpreting pop tunes of his day like billie holiday did for hers, and those sounds wind softly through the house, gently seeking and unerringly finding a receptive ear, a welcoming soul

every breath costs some amount of air, sometimes the breathing is painfully evident like the labor of inhaling while running three miles atop the levee five or six mornings out of the week, other times the dues is less obvious: like we can't enjoy our separate lives and simultaneously be together all the time, sometimes i like to read in the same room you are sitting in doing whatever you're doing. other times i'm far away, far, far, away

i could never have written a poem like this twenty years ago, not enough distance to look back and see that the horizon is not just an ever receding, unreachable horizontal line in front of me but also a lengthily, spherical curve that wraps behind, knotted by contradictions and smoothed by the resolution of holding what i can grasp and of letting go what i can't hold

AS SERIOUS AS A HEART ATTACK

i have never been fully domesticated
but i have been civilized

by women taught that the heart
is more than a muscle

a life drum whose function is
both physical blood pumping
and spiritual longing to be embraced

but love, ah love is a river
we may get wet
but we can never drink it all
love always flows on
more than we can ever swallow

no matter how thirsty
we claim to be

bb explains why…

we'd be so damn mean
if me and lucille couldn't
sing these sad ass songs

Been Here & Gone (a love letter found thrown up in a Mississippi cottonfield)

I love you
But
I'm gone, loves all yall
—yeah, even you Lil Joe with your worthless ass—

I'm going to miss
Us laughing and joking
Wrestling with each other
Arguing about who fart the loudest
And how long church gon last next Sunday

Yeah, I know, I don't go no mo
But that don't mean I ain't gonna miss it

I didn't tell nobody I was going
Cause I didn't want to get none of yall
Who I most care about in no trouble
Still and all, I'm sho nuff gonna miss yall
But I gots to go

I broke my hoe and left it
In two pieces shaped like an X
Down by the hanging oak
Yall know the tree I'm talking about

They ain't gonna lynch me
Might have to kill me if they catch me
But ain't no rope for this man's neck
Momma, I loves you especial
You too daddy, Lord knows how you was
Strong enough to stand staying in 'Sippi

Pa you mo man that me
I gots to go
I can't take it

I ain't much for words so there ain't much mo
For me to say. Don't take my few little mumbles
To mean there ain't a whole bunch of feelings
Up in my heart. I know I'm repeating myself
But I loves all yall
It's just
I got to go

Eartha Ann please don't hate me for not staying
We talked about it before, you said
When Big Joe snuck off, Eartha you said
You could never leave your peoples behind
Like that, said specially not Big Momma
On account she 84 and it might kill her
To see you fly away… Eartha I miss your arms
And everything already
And I ain't hardly gone good
I guess what it is, is that I can swallow missing
But I can't stand staying

So that's it
I loves yall
Miss yall
Been here and done gone

Bro/therLove

my brothers & i used to fight each other
giving no quarter, striking where it hurts deepest
like raking a fork cross the soft vinyl grooves
of Sketches of Spain

i still have scars on my hand
from a knife slice, on the other hand
i saved my brother's life one night
by stilling his tongue as he fought
through an asthma/sinus seizure

as men we have all three gone our separate ways
though our paths continue to cross
& i see them sometimes looking & sounding
like inola in her efficient dignity
or ferd with his country wit of words

> "the work ain't hard
> & the boss ain't mean,
> you ain't got nothing to complain abt"

each of us is who we are
& all of us are a little bit of each other
surprisingly sweet & not infrequently gentle
in our burly ninth ward blackness

catch us on those rare occassion when we are three
in one place & the circus might as well shut down

my brothers & i used to fight each other fiercely
& now matured in the afterglow of battle, we realize
that all three of us share the sacred crown
of hardwon brotherlove.

COSMIC DEPUTY

as a cosmic deputy
of the great goodness of life
you will be required to
taste the electricity of the most shocking midnight,
kiss the totality of experiences and imaginations,
chew deeply into both the reality and repercussions
of your every human gesture, whether sweet or sour,
conscious or simply a knee-jerk reaction
to the assault of truths we are underprepared
to understand or acknowledge
upon first encountering incomprehensible newness

should you accept this pro bono position
you will be expected
to take unfading mental snapshots of each sunset,
to gleefully give joy at the drop of a hat, and,
without rancor, to understand that being done wrong
is the inevitable price of the ticket
for participating in a feature length festival
of symbiotic existence on planet earth,
additionally, you must agree
never to take your marbles and your ball and go
running home just because we are losing

all cosmic deputies must commit
a minimum of fifty-five
random acts of kindness a day, must be
unceasing in freely offering
unprovoked displays of beauty, must
never sell what should be given, never buy what
ought be bartered and never talk when hip music
is being played, all deputies are expected
to take off their clothes in the presence of love

and volunteer community service by providing
aid and sustenance to young trees, to ancestors
known and unknown, and to wave in drivers
who are trying to cut in front of you
on the expressway, always remember
it is better to masturbate than fuck over someone

at this time, i ask each individual
who is prepared to give the day a glorious name
and to arouse each night to passionate blushes
to please rise and be sworn in

it is customary for those who remain seated
to laugh, hoot and make jokes about
how dumb someone has to be to agree to respect
all forms of life: plant, animal, and even human
additionally, at appropriate moments non-deputies
may even fart to express your indignation
at having to be in the presence and proximity
of people who think that pulling down a fat profit
is a piss poor way to make a living

will those who are ready to deeply drink
from the well of the great goodness
of life please stand & raise your left hand,
the one closest to your heart,
& repeat after me

> i promise
> to always strive
> to become better than i am,
> to admit my general ignorance,
> and to realize that even a dog turd
> can teach me how to grow things,

furthermore,
of my own free will
and without coercion of any sort
i agree to question all authorities,
accept no dogmas,
and reject any ideology
that does not make babies laugh

i understand
that in the cosmic context
my life is both
quantitatively insignificant
and qualitatively pivotal
to the maintenance
of all things good and beautiful

in the name of earth,
wind,
water
and fire
in the nurturing of the mother,
the spirit of the father,
and with the innocence
of a baby
i profess my profound belief
that the propagation
and elevation
of life
is the only thing
worth dying for

i pronounce you a cosmic deputy
of the great goodness of life
you may now take a deep breath
and come out smiling

CONGO SQUARE

the oumas indians prepared this place for us
centuries before our arrival
a sacred spot where corn festivals
were celebrated & as the colonializers came
they pushed aside our hosts
& introduced us in chains
& by the late 1700s we somehow
recognizing the sacredness of le place de congo,
we somehow, and the how of our persuasive methodologies
is not clear at this moment, but nevertheless,
even as slaves we crafted and created a space
where we could be free to be we
and thusly we countered the sacrilegiousness of the french
giving great homage to our ancestors as well as
giving praise & thanx to our red blooded brothers & sisters

this is an oral libational toast
to congo square
to native americans
to our ancestors
who made a circle in a square
and gave us a way to stay ourselves save ourselves
from the transformatory ugliness of america
which refuses to recognize the spirituality of life
and celebrates death with crosses & crosses, double
& triple crosses, the middle passage the first cross,
christianity the double cross and capitalism
the ultimate triple coup de grace cross of our captivity

but the terror of crosses notwithstanding
we sang, we beat, we be, we was & is
hail, congo square
our african gods have not been obliterated

they have merely retreated inside
the beat of us until we are ready
to release them into a world that we
re-create, a world heralded by the beat
be, beat being, beating being
of black heart drums

heart beat heart beat heart be/at this place
at this place be heart beat be we
beating place in new world space
beating being in place
in new world preserving our ancient pace
our dance is the god walk
our music, the god talk

first thing we do, let's get together
circle ourselves into community
no beginning no end connected together
and singing ringing singing
in a ring

second let's be original
aboriginal / be what we were before
we became what we are, be bamboula
dance, be banza music, and sing song words
which have no english translation

third let us remember
never to forget even when we can't remember
the specifics we must retain the essentials
the bounce the blood flow the feel the spirit
grow energy, must retain and pass on
the essential us-ness that
others want to dissipate whip out of us
but no matter how much of us they prohibit

deep inside us is us
remains us inside
& needs only
the beat
to set
us free

the beat to free us

it is morning, a sun day, a field w/out shade but dark
with the people black of us in various shades
eclipsing the sun with our elegance

we are centuries later now
and still this sacred ground calls us
to remember / to beat / to be

beat CONGO SQUARE be CONGO SQUARE
beat be beat be
remember

Dinner With Jerry

(for Dr. Jerry Ward)

those of us who understand the magnitude
of being deeply serious
in our life endeavors, who truly
comprehend the inevitability
of errors, the fickleness of chance
the utter impossibility of practical predictions
especially when one has learned to consider
the always ironic hilarity
of unintended consequences mocking
even our most reverent work

those of us who have been buffeted,
battered and weathered
as a result of our considerable strengths
in resisting mundane but copious
systemic bullshit and yet we continue
undeterred in our task of midwifing
human kindness toward one and others
as we shrug off the defeats, setbacks
and god ugly reverses
nastying so much of what passes
for daily life among colleagues and also
among other creatures

of passing acquaintance

those of us humble enough to accept
toiling without any where near equitable
compensation or even a modicum of real
recognition

we are the ones who share
sunlight and shade with each other
small moments of beauty
when the weather is warm
the sun crepuscularly soft
the soup appropriately body temperature
for easy savoring
and the salad greens freshly gathered
with attractive garnishments of strawberry

those of us briefly basking amid
the conviviality of obscure references
and intellectual challenges including
brusque and sometimes bawdy
critiques of certain bureaucracies, peers,
politicians and other opponents
among the plethora of fools
who unfortunately not only dot our
social landscapes, but also (and
inopportunely for us) some of them
have even attained positions of social
architect and other levels of authority

those of us who can deal with all of this
and still continue to carve out an hour or two
a week to have our breaths embrace
as we taste the vintage sweetness
of our wry humor and the tangy sharpness
of our withering sarcasm
we are the ones
who will never die nor despair
for lack of love

even though despair is not an unknown taste
and death but a few doors down
the remaining years of our earthly existence

nevertheless, we know an intimate
human eternalness mined from real love
shared with a fellow traveler

as we press on in our pilgrimage
passing through these trying days and times
marking the cosmic calendar of our lives

Echoing Eshu's Love Songs

(for "eshu" ethelbert miller)

man, the relevance of coincidence is a motherfucker
just today, walked down commercial street
the business end of provincetown
in and out of shops, paused here, there
entered where attracted by something
backed out and continued
found this used bookstore (found?
must be careful of my verbs
i am not a white man
the store was there before i
got there) entered
they had a poetry bookcase
bought 4 books: sam cornish—songs
of jubilee, kimiko hahn—air pocket,
akua lezli hope—embouchure, and
e. ethelbert miller—where
are the love poems
for dictators? / before midnight
had read, scanned or run thru
them all. yes, of course
i knew about dictators,
have run into a few before
on an occasion or two
or should i say ill-occasion
have even been one, but
i did not own the book on that

there are no love songs
for dictators, not even
i'll be glad when you're dead

you rascal you—cause even that
has a bit of affection, anyway
i think it one of your better books

you were on to something
or maybe simply on something
or was it someone
who had your mind so open
you could feel the impress
of another's smile, another's
grimace, and you could walk that
shit home backwards and blind
like a beggar going back and forth
between their favorite corner
and the poor piece of space
they call home

so, then i got this email from you. and all i can say is damn, and look out the window a second into the dark and know that either god is laughing or i should be because the universe sure enough knows how to confound the wisdom of we poor wretched fools who make the mistake of trying to understand it, the universe, that is, and i started to wondering if anyone ever really knows why their lover loves them, actually that's not quite true, cause where i started with was wondering does nia know why i love her, do i know, is love knowable or simply, if we are lucky, embraceable? like who knows where the song comes from or goes to, we just lucky when we can hit the notes and carry a tune …like that, and now i'm free typing this without knowing where it's coming from or where i will end up, just knowing i wanted to let you know, that i hear you, brother, i hear your songs and echo the rhythms—ain't no love song for dictators, for love is beyond the frequency of the ears of those who consciously hurt others

even death will not stop me from struggling

i will continue
as ashes & dust

my bronze flesh will join the soil
of free lands everywhere
& grow trees
be the mud within which rabbits burrow
be carpet of rain forest mountain walls
 welcoming gorillas home

my bronze flesh
sacred ground
will become ancestor soil

and i will also be dry dust
refusing to cover despots
i'll clog the air filters
of tanks & invade the nostrils
of invaders

you hear that wind
that's my dying breath
laughing at those who thought
they'd seen the last of me

you see that baby eating soil
dirt smeared around her cheeks
that worker dusting himself off
that couple of love embracing on
 picnic ground
that hopi sand painting
that amazonian stripped with the chalk
 of white clay
you see me

i am sorry to disappoint you
but i do not die
i just move to another plane of existence
and become the fertilizer of the future

even when i'm gone
i will still be here
though death do us part

exit left

when i came to i didn't know where i was
on the ground, prone, near the levee bottom—i blacked out
while jogging, got up, walked home, still laboring a bit
between deep gulps i told nia as much as i could remember

my brother is a cardiologist, nia urged me to call him
tuesday morning early i take an ekg and the results are so
    disturbing
keith schedules me for a battery of tests an hour and a half later
i still have a meeting to do in between, my blood pressure was
    normal

i reappear, am radioactively injected, get wired up and climb on
a treadmill, lay under a nuclear camera, chat as though nothing
was wrong, submit to a sonogram, nia is there the whole time,
the results are negative, acceptable, i did not have a heart attack

keith can not determine the etiology of the alarming ekg
but i know the hard truth: at fifty i am almost through
i am dying and perhaps there is a metaphysical reason
no physical break down showed up on the machines this time
as the world unravels around me i coolly center the resulting
    chaos
within the calm of my karma's core—this is how i exist: i dare to do
all the good i can, i accept the unevenness of chance, i simply love
life for what it is and when my time comes, i am not afraid to
exit

Flying Over America

i'm flying home
flying, flying, flying, flying
flying home

this, ancient land was once not uniform but free to be
whatever the sun shone upon
not furrowed by industry
nor ribboned by concrete
but simply a life path
trod by bare and moccasined feet

now from coast to coast
from great lakes to gulf
there is the mechanical roar of engines
the boom of bombs
the staccato stutter of hand guns
the quiet binary clicking of computers, and
the tortured cry of nature writhing
twisted by modernity

i am an African encased in aviated metal
surrounded by the sad contentment
of civilized progress anxious to maintain
its hegemony of coercion
as we fly forward into the future
unmindful of the defecation we leave behind

intermittently dozing i dream
of appreciating the simple silence
of a heavy metal epoch rusting to dust
of meditating in the amber
of a muted spangled banner song

this land we jet across was ancient once
and though i know we can never again
atavistically return home
into a nostalgic past, still i long
to see this soil be ancient once more

unmolested
by a social order so unrepentant
in its disdain
for the womb
of our earthly environment
that only its death
can justify the manifest destiny
of this nation's existence

only death
can possibly cover the debt &
repay the cost of creating
this hubristic nation state
which so wantonly & methodically murdered red,
so avariciously & cruelly enslaved black

if this is truly one nation under god
then surely their god must be a devil

FOR LIFE / FOR MAISHA

i love
you & have
nothing but encouragement
for yr life in my missive to you,
yr life, not mine, what you see & be,
how you shape yr space & escape
from the restrictions earlier generations
have created, over their walls
into the wilderness yes, but free
free, & that's the real, to be free
to be everything or nothing like
what has been artificially erected
by those who want young people
to be old images, regurgitated thoughts,
& rather stupendously stupid
reincarnations of realities
this world would have been
oh so much better off without
such twisted combinations

you know
& i know you may not know
where you're going to
but you know
you're never going back to
those bruising and battering befores,
those false images of stability enforced by fists or
incapacitating inhibitions
& above all, never back to pick up on
all that emotional baggage
standing on every corner
of the small town called crescent city

it is so difficult to be young in this old world
so strange, so frustrating trying to find community
when every individual thinks
they are a king or a queen
or for sure that you should be their slave or knave
co-dependent or some other
reduction ad absurdum

there are firing squads outside,
paddy rollers in the woods
ghosts riders in the sky
& a million good reasons to stay
holed up inside, be careful but don't be afraid
even if you can't find the key to the combination
at least climb out the window and keep going
the only way to be really free is to never surrender

so that's it, this letter is to let you know
not everybody back here wants you back
as a little brown girl
reliving what never happened anyway
except as some male orchestrated fantasy
& i guess that is the essence—
since life is real and finite—
if you are going to be somebody's fantasy
you might as well live & be yr own dreams
regardless of the cost or
how you may lose yr way sometimes,
live & be, live yr dreams & be yrself
however difficult or confusing it may be to discover
yr life lived to the fullest is the best & only
value you can give to a world already overflowing
with frightened and repressed children dressed up
in adult years, live & be maisha, live & be
yrself

FORCES OF NATURE: HOPE SONG

/para Steph & Percival/

do not be bound by your mind
you are more than your thoughts

we don't just trod down time
mere materialist bricks of sod

we are immanent energy
both of & from the earth

our breath is wind
our flesh is soil

each smile an array
of sun warmth

each tear a droplet
of dew

but there is also another world
which animates us

delve into the forest
of your emotions

squat before the fire
of your imagination

sleep with the reality
of your dreams

our spirit surge is
stronger than computers

the dialectic
of human touch & feelings

an endless motor
self recycling

in the manner of oceans feeding
clouds & rain replenishing sea

while our being is as definite
as the texture of rocks

our mellifluous souls
are majestic

as the stoic millennium
of mountains

our essence is
two in one

both an awesome
aspect of nature

& a spiritual
projection

of life's
creative force

FREEDOM—A Haitian Rant

After we ran our oppressors into the sea
You have since never tired trying to run us into the ground

After the earth opened its jaws to swallow us
Your assistance rushed in to bury us

You say we can not govern, our government is corrupt
Who kidnapped Aristide, the president we elected, a priest
who made our world work and not simply prayed for miracles,
in fact, we elected him twice, and twice you took your guns and
made him leave and would not let us vote for anything he
    represented—
our government is not corrupt, corrupt is the government you
    put in
our president's place, our government is in exile

You swear we are not capable of caring for ourselves, perhaps
We are too busy servicing your sex tourists, making your mickey
    mouse
clothes, and sewing your balls you love to play with

You say everyone envies your freedom
Yet it was our soldiers who saved George Washington's ass
in Savannah when you were fighting for your freedom but
you never give us credit for helping to create your freedom
and worse yet when you got your precious freedom you did not
give freedom to all your citizens—we in Haiti were the first truly
free country in all of the Americas, everyone was declared free
in our new republic, everyone red, black, white, yellow or brown—
no one was a slave in free Haiti, it took you almost a century
to free your enslaved people, yes not until 1865
did you even halfway declare all your male citizens as Haiti
was free on day one of our birth (tell me I am wrong

but I believe you did not let women vote until 1920)
no one who knows our history envies your 2/5 free history

You say we are poor but when will you give us back the money
you sent marines to steal from us in 1915 when you invaded us
and took over our banks,
no matter how long a thief keeps what he stole,
no matter how many generations gone,
he is still a thief, which is why
one of your presidents, the paedophile Jefferson who
took up with a thirteen year old, famously said:
when I think that god is just, I tremble
for the fate of my country
When we think that god is just, we just smile
and pray the day of reckoning will soon come,
beautiful as a Jacmel sunrise

We are Haitian, we love freedom
who are you and what do you love?

GATHERING SPEED
(a single sister thinks before she leaps)

these things take
time, ya know
time to root
time to grow
these things do

winter can be so long some
times, no sun, no
rain, just bare cold against
bare soul when we shiver
like solitary leafless tree,
a wind twisted silhouette
on well traveled urban street
silently struggling to continue
the search for some other spring

deep within my eye space
resides resilient spirit
which seeks to sing but
in the stillness
of a frozen silence
such songs take time
to sound

yes, most mornings
we want to feel music
yet even our sleep spots
are cool to the touch
as our palms smooth the sheets
of our single beds that
we make up, and we
empty our heads of hope, while

sleepwalking through a
mandated hibernation from which
to awaken and live dreams is
both dangerous and difficult

besides
the last. . . well, the last, i
mean i was just thinking
about how these things
takes time, time to forget
how i felt
when the last love check bounced, what
am i saying?

for seven months
i went to work
and went home
and went out with friends,
friends whom i love, but
friends who are not lovers
and watched television
and read the paper
and ate and exercised and
i read a novel, read
two novels, read three
novels, a book of short
stories, several books
of poetry – i don't even
really like poetry – and i
watched television

excuse me
i can not trust you
these things take, what
i really mean is i

can not trust me, my mouth
is liable to talk, to kiss

i am not a slave
to desire, nor do i
love pain, i do not
want to hurt anymore
i wish these things
did not take so long

i try not to expect any
thing of you, i try to just
take it as it comes

why do you even want to
talk to me
or is it that you think
just because i'm alone
it will be easy to take
me, easy to have your way
with me without love

if i say this to you
will you be angry with me

why, really, why do you
want to talk to me
these things take time
ya know
time to root
time to grow

he gets off at 4:30 / it's 6:09 now

here...

an unencumbered softness
my naked breast / taste me

the luminous curve of crimson
lips eager to flutter
across bearded dark fullness / kiss me

the form fitting expectancy
of tense eager arms / embrace me

a moist tangled crescent
immodestly blanketing
my fertility / enter me

none of me is mine
all of me is yours

here am i / where are you?

I AM A POET

Some know me as a fire-breather, I
have armed nuclear warheads, traveled
around this troubled albeit beautiful
planet, I am culturally bilingual (music
is my mother tongue) but thru
my lyrics I seek other tongues, dance
to other rhythms, the other is also me, I

know that I must know the whole
world in order to fully be my whole
self, indeed, the sun and the universe
are my ancestry, after all my physical is
the stuff of stars, I am
black, my eyes are capable
of seeing the entire spectrum of light
especially the invisible, the night

my consciousness is the interior
of seeds, my subject matter is subversive
my mission is to go beyond
myself, to eventually become one
with everyone else, even enjoin and transform
my enemies, to grasp

and understand the totality of
existence, politics is only one
letter of my alphabet, love is my real
rosetta stone, do not be
surprised when i turn up in a drop
of ocean spray, a baby's giggle, the
singing of Sirius stars, nothing
nor any one is foreign to me
i am everything both known and

especially all that is
unknown

I don't want to live anywhere where they are killing me

1.
it's crazy. most of us
kind of assume that where we are born
is home, where our first kiss was, learning to walk, literally,
throwing our first stone at someone in anger,
sitting at the table a mouth full of mother's meatloaf
or was it strawberry pie, or even monkey bread—
those twisted strings of dough that were a wonderful
combination of chewy cake and sweet stuffing—
catching the bus home from school with friends,
the first drink, wasn't it when uncle teddy
served you beer at thanksgiving, you were five?
like that, we think of that location in the mythic sense

the high drama that came later, the desperately sought
trysts, sneaking to liaison with someone you know you
ought to avoid, or the first time you got together
with someone whom you wanted the whole world
to know you were committed to being with for life,
or so you thought, how wonderful the world looked
as you lay dreaming on your back your head
secure in a special someone's lap, or how short
the walk after the dance from the club to the parking lot,
what you wouldn't have given for a reprise of that heaven
the way a lover looks when their whole face smiles
just because you came around the corner with
a yellow tulip in your hand and a pack of almond m&m's
secreted behind your back as you whispered
smokey's ooh baby baby into an eagerly awaiting ear

actually those were the preludes—the real high drama
came some years later, the first time calling someone,
anyone, to come and get you out of jail, which you were in

for doing something stupid, something really, really
stupid, and then there was the accident when you banged
up someone's new car, but those were just the breaks, not
the actual high drama of sitting sullen in some counselor's
waiting room, your head thrown back to the wall
avoiding the eyes of your better half who was now
the loyal opposition and whose eyes were the same eyes
only smaller in the head of the child to whom you
could not some how find the right words to make sense
of this mess that was formerly your marriage

where these scenes take place, the parlor in which
a cousin's camera has caught you crying, the foggy mirror
where you examined yourself, one flight up in a total
stranger's house and sheepishly you wonder what were you
doing in this blue tiled bathroom so very early in the morning
when you were supposed to be somewhere else—life is what
some people call this, and where you live your life, shouldn't
that be the place you call home?

2.
the water. my god the water. the angry water
rain roaring sideways with the force of a freight train,
smashing your resolve to ride it out, or inching
down an interstate at two miles an hour so call evacuating
from the water. the dirty, angry water, running
if you were lucky enough to have wheels and a wallet
with plastic in it. the water. you will dream of
wet mountains falling on you and wake up gasping
for air as though you were drowning, oh the water
deeper than any pool you've ever swam in,
water more terrible than anything you can think
of, another middle passage, except this time
they don't even provide ships

I used to wonder how my ancestors survived
the Atlantic, Katrina has answered that question,
I wonder no more—there is a faith that is beyond
faith, a belief when there is nothing left to believe in,
no, not god, well, yes, god, for some, for many, it was
jesus, a few hamdullahed, or whatever, but it was also
whatever that visited this terror upon us, and so
to keep believing in whatever, now takes something
the mind can not imagine, the realization that in order
to live you had to survive and in order to survive
you had to do whatever needed to be done, few
of us really, really know what we will do
when we've got nothing but have to find something
to keep us going, how you manage your sanity
in the water, corpses floating by, gas flames
bubbling up from some leaking underground line,
and you sitting on a roof and you just pissed
on yourself because, well, because there was
no where to go and do your business, five days
of filth, no water but flood water, no food but
hot sun, no sanitation but being careful where
you stepped, where you slept, where you turned
your back and eliminated, being careful to survive

twelve days later and you still don't know where
all your family is, if you've got faith, you're about to
use it all—is this some of what our ancestors saw?

3.
it is over a month later and you still can't walk
on the land that used to be your backyard,
they treat you like a tourist, you can only
be driven down your street in a big bus,
you can only look out the window at what twisted,

funk encrusted little remains of all you ever owned
and some kid with a gun won't let you go
to get big mama's bible

this shit is fucked up, that's what it is,
fucked up and foul, the smell of a million
toilets overflowing, of food that been rotting
for days inside a refrigerator that became
an oven because the electricity was off and
the sun was beaming down ninety degrees or more

and the worse part is that none of what you
already went through is the worst part, the worst
is yet to come as government peoples with
boxes and things they stick into the ground
tell you that even if the water hadn't drowned
you, something called toxicity has made it
impossible for you to stay here, they are
telling you it is impossible for you to stay
in the house that been in your family
for over fifty years even though it's still standing
it's impossible to live here, and what shall
we call this? what shall we tell the children
when they ask: when are we going home?

4.
I don't want to live anywhere where they have
tried to kill us even if it was once a place
I called home—but still and all, my bones
don't cotton to Boston, I can't breath
that thinness they call air in Colorado,
a Minnesota snow angel don't mean shit
to me, and still and all, even with all of that,
all the many complaints that taint my

appreciation of charity, help and shelter,
even though I know there is no turning back
to drier times, still, as still as a fan when
the man done cut the 'lectric off, still,
regardless of how much I hate the taste
of bland food, still, I may never go back,
not to live, maybe for a used to be
visit, like how every now and then you
go by a graveyard… I am not bitter, I am
just trying to answer the question:
what is life without a home?
what is life, without
a home? and how long does it take
to grow a new one?

i have my mother's hands

though cancer claimed
my mother's body decades ago
inola's reincarnation remains within me
a deeply treasured and unerring auditor—
an inquisitive, music loving child
with eyes wide bright and earth brown
whose trusting reach upthrusting
to clasp a helping man's hand
unclenches the maleness of my fist
and continually causes my essence
to cup the strength of masculine fingers
into the soft of a flesh spoon
emulating and saluting the feminine
gesture of giving unconditionally

I Look But What Is There To See?

look
ing for
you is like
standing
on the track
staring at the space

left

by a slow train
what done long
gone

around the bend

only
the whistle sound
faintly
in the air

and the ground's
vibration
felt down
to your toes

nothing

more.

I Stare Into The Air

I came to see you
Did you know I was there?

I don't think so. Your head was
Back, your mouth wide open,
Your eyes closed. The sound
Of the machines was louder
Than your labored breathing.

I thought of Picasso, how he painted
That horse, it pained me
That you looked like a wounded animal.
I know you were knocked out—morphine

Morphine is not medicine
That's what they give to you when
They don't know what else to do.

About three or four hours later
We returned and now you were awake,
Or at least your eyes were open

I held your hand, lightly, I did not want
To hurt you so I was careful
With my touch and my jokes

I knew you couldn't laugh. That hurt
Me too. I will never forget the deep
Rumble of your laughter, how your
Eyes would glow, how laugh lines
Were all over your expansive face
You would even reach out and slap
My shoulder but not that day. All

You did was blink to let me know
That you heard me, that you knew
I came to visit you the weekend
Before you died.

I went home glad to have seen you
Sad to have seen you like that

Almost exactly one week later
The call early in the morning did not
Surprise me. I did not cry. I wanted
To. I did not curse. I should
Have. I did not do anything except
Sit back in my chair and stare
Into the nothingness of the air
In front of me.

I Thought Of This As I Passed In The Hallway And You Looked Up While Drying Off After Stepping Out Of Your Sunday Shower

in a lover's eye one can see something, perhaps, a glint of the potent
beauty we all long to be when we giddily cast our fate to the whims
of desire, and even if we have never pranced high stepping at the front
of satisfaction's parade most of us have nevertheless stood close
enough to the drumming to reflect the shudder of sensuality coiled
within the trembling of impatient flesh awaiting the release of touch

who needs to apologize for feeling good, for opening the soul
to the bliss experience, especially when we consider our hearts
observe neither stopwatch nor timetable upon tasting the sincerity
sweet of a tear or two when a special person voluntarily confesses
their resolve to attempt to be better than the frailty we all inevitably are
whenever carrying the ball of contradictions commonly called love

in this briefness we transubstantiate, visit the angelic state whose reaching
we humans are capable of grasping but oh so seldom achieve

I Want To Talk About You

(for my sister Czerny)

this poem was supposed to be
for/abt you but as i was thinking
i felt another need
& know in order to truth talk
abt you i had to truth talk
abt how our hours
on this earth spot
some call a civilized nation
has been bitter centuries long
long, long after the chains fell
our unhealed scars are serious sores
still too tender to touch

abt how few
of us really comprehend the enormity
of our history of captivity
not only the horror of what was done to us
but what the residue of that historic undoing
continues to do to us today

our genitals were
put on public display

if you were white
you could see cleotis' thing
silent in a sealed see-through coffin
howard kept the sinister cylinder at his shop
behind the unpainted cypress wood counter
out of plain sight but was always proud
to hoist the mason jar
with the shriveled, pickled penis

into the surprise of sunlit delight
and the carefree hoots of the gathered
good old boys, although we never knew
who actually did the cutting
we all knew where the evidence was kept

they say in france they got
the vagina of our sister entombed
(for medical research of course)
venus, the "hottentot venus"
they sarcastically called her,
and when she was alive they paraded her
naked on a pay per view basis
and people paid to see how big her butt
was, and later after she died, how big
her vagina was, and the worse
part was that crowds of humans
actually went and oohed and ahhed
and paid money to see something
the creator gave to all of us

could my name be cleotis
could your name be venus
& why should anyone want
to trophy our genitals?

i turn over naked
in my nude sleep sometimes,
hold myself hard with my hand
and imagine the pain
and wonder how does a man
live without himself?

what i really want to talk abt
is how we lived despite

the mutilations
i am so impressed by the beauty
of a people who can survive
the public display of our privates,
who could rise the next morning
face the pain and still believe
in living a good life

you are one of those old ones
the women who tear-washed
and bare-handedly buried the broken bodies
cauterized wounds and stitched together
some kind of tough, tough love
that mended men
and raised the manchild even after
the man was gone

this poem is
for you and all the race
women like you who continue
to feed us reason to live
when suicide seems unavoidably sensible

me and all my manhood
bears daily witness
i would be nothing were it not
for the redemptive love
of certain of my sisters, my mothers
my aunts, grandmothers and
women friends securely umbilicaling
sustenance into my soul

all the remaining years of my life
i will never cease
wanting to talk abt you

needing to talk abt you
to talk abt you
talk abt you

I WONDER WHAT YOU FEEL LIKE NOW

(after a 24nov2010 meeting
with Ozge Ersoy & her friend Canay)

I talked to Esim yesterday, had not seen her since
March 1965 when I was fleeing back south, Ozge you were
The Esim I seldom recall but can never forget

The patience of Esim's eyes speaking to me full on unafraid
Of my young blackness, like when you slapped my hand
As I moved to caress the magnet that was your breast

And shortly after the sting had subsided and I withdrew
My fingers from beneath your blouse I felt your hand atop
Mine leading me to cup your fully clothed breast

I was not confused, I knew that we were reaching
For each other across dangerous cultural waters, Esim
Bozoklar from Turkey, Val Ferdinand from New Orleans

Most days I think our union never could have held
I had too many changes yet to go through, too much
Growth to accomplish, too much, besides America is always

Both inhospitable and dangerous for any shade
Of otherness, any language other, and especially
Any mixture or matching of outsiders, would I

Like Baldwin have flown to Turkey, how would our children
Have identified themselves—Esim, though we chose not to
Cross those tough bridges I think our conversation perhaps

Assures me there was room for us on the other side, Ozge
You could have been my daughter and Esim's eyes
Would be the answer to questions we have for each other

A Turkish woman is talking to me tenderly even though
A casual ease-dropper might simply think us intellectuals
In a café exchanging ideas and academic theories

The onlooker would not, could not feel the river of emotions
Flowing beneath the calm of our conversation, Esim/Ozge
I don't know what you were thinking about, but I'm certain

I know that I was thinking about you; and now I am writing this
A day later on another day like most days except today is the last
Thursday in November when America celebrates a holiday

Giving thanks for all they stole, most of us render praises unto
The lord but shouldn't our hosannas be devil due? Fortunately
I don't believe in all of that, any of that, I believe

In life in all its contradictions, I try to avoid absolutes
And sentimentalities, regrets and maudlin thoughts about
Could have beens, should have beens, and any thing other

Than what is—nevertheless I wonder, Esim, are you still alive,
Do you reside anywhere besides inside this cup of memory
Harbored in the flesh of my hand's long ago touch

It Is Raining

the rain comes down very slow
& consults with the night
& brightens the sidewalks,
& makes allusions to a beautiful feeling inside;
i see it
& imagine some magnificent slow dance we do

all over the air is getting good,
the raindrops are making curious
cross rhythms on the window panes
it is raining; thinking of you

Janis Joplin/poor white refuse refugee running for cover of rock.

like a baby with an hereditary
birth defect, i didn't ask
for this white skin privilege;
this maximum security
with guards everywhere
and the wall so far off
so high, so hard to scale
minefields of twinkling consumables
studding the distance between
me and the rest of humanity,
a spiraling bob of drugs at the top

and i ain't asking for no
mercy neither, no pity, none
of yall tears, anyway,
i'm going to kill myself
or at least die trying

they say i'm so wild
cause all what i need is a man,
a real man, a hard on
but like once a man was in me
and said "god, you so ugly
i can't look" but so what
is his opinion anyway but
a thirty second tv commercial
he thinks he's a man
he thinks niggers stink
he thinks i'm a piece of meat
he's my father, my brother
and this is no gentle incest
nor any human touch

so i will do these insane acts
i will sing in the night
say what i want
drink and be driven crazy
put a tombstone
and real flowers on
a black woman's grave
and have no regrets, no
regrets

kalamu looks at lil val,* fifty-five years later

I sit there staring
A bright, candy-striped ball balanced in my right hand
I have on short pants
My five year old eyes
—I have no glasses yet—stare
Unblinking into the future

Boy, you have no idea what's coming
round tomorrow's bend
you can not imagine
you're less than two years away
from choking on your grandfather's
cigar butt discarded in your grandmother's rose garden
and vowing never again to smoke

one of the few promises you've kept
throughout adulthood—but then even in your innocence
you were wise enough to forgo any predictions
other than to be true to yourself

is that why you will leave your first wife

don't just sit there, say something

do you remember who took this picture of you
and why, what it was someone wanted to remember
about you, fifty-five years from now
you will look at this picture in your mind
and vainly attempt to connect all the dots
into a coherence that reality
always subverts

* My birth name was Vallery Ferdinand III. My father was known as Big Val and I, of course, was…

vallery, if you saw me now
would you recognize kalamu or would you
wonder who is he and what is he to you?

locks

to shape the world is every man's desire
a drive that phallically fashions the ultimate
tool of possession—i was fumbling to unlock
the front door when i realized: these jingling
surrogate penises were the keys guarding whatever
material i have been taught to think of as mine

who constructed the key? my mind flips: i remember
visiting tanzania, inside a traditional structure
no lock no bars no closet no safe
and what about chastity belts?

i am amazed to realize how much of society
is based on the human body filtered through
the gender bias of patriarchy protecting
the ownership of what they claim is theirs

MING THE MERCILESS—OUR FIELD GENERAL

We knew her as Ming The Merciless
Our nom de guerre for Oretha Castle Haley
Who fiercely led us into battle, often
Against foes we didn't know secretly opposed us

When I was but a handful of years out of short pants
I was the eleventh grader sitting in at Woolworth's
Under Ming's guidance, an ardent warrior against segregation
Ask Mr. Schwegmann, whose lunch counter we confronted
At his new store off Chef Menteur & Paris Road
Along the Industrial Canal in the vast Ninth Ward
The future home turf of the SOUL Civil&Silver Rights
    organization
Eventually co-led by the Weasel (Sherman Copelin)
And the Bear (Don Hubbard), a CORE veteran,
It took the cunning and brawn of the two of them to match
Oretha's insightful social and political maneuverings
Schwegmann's heavy, brown paper supermarket bags
Were much sought for a politician's slogan or smiling face
As those shopping bags were familiar to many a voter as well
As to school students who religiously used them
To cover their textbooks—some of us even drew big, bold
Purple and crimson declarations of love
Full of intertwining red hearts and roses
As in Alfred loves Angela on those beige bags

The major avenue for Black retail shopping, Dryades Street
Was renamed Oretha Castle Haley Boulevard in her honor
But long before the name change she was already
Seeing around corners most of us didn't know
We would have to turn in the course of our long march
Toward long sought political freedom and economic equality

Ming declared public education a major battlefield
A fight we ultimately loss in the new millennium
When New Orleans no longer has any public schools left
Under the democratically elected school board's direction,
The rapacious bandits of privatizing education
Are making a killing commandeering the charter movement
And essentially foreclosing one of only two
Major political/economic foundations of our Black Community
—Containers on ocean-going ships
Destroyed the longshoremen's union, indeed, I literally
Almost cried when I saw the ILA (International Longshoremen's
Association Hall) falling beneath a wrecking ball, after all
That auditorium was where we Blacks held civic meetings
And proms, concerts and dances, were Otis sang a simple song
And the Royal Dukes of Rhythm played complex big band
Arrangements for our dancing and listening enjoyment
But beyond the merriment stood an institution that
Literally supplied both money and manpower for our
Sixties and Seventies uprising that not only led to numerous
Gigantic gatherings: sports activities, and a plethora of
Conclaves, conventions and exhibitions from the Sugarbowl and
Superbowl to gun shows and automobile roundups
But also supplied economic incentives and a cornucopia of
Money making opportunities, especially for Superdome Services
Inc.
A purveyor of maintenance, janitorial, and event staffing
Headed by the Weasel and the Bear, the duo had moved
From political brokerage to economic development

Between the school teachers and the longshoremen
And all the institutions that were thereby supported,
From corner stores to mansions in the newly developed
New Orleans East, where else could we go, where else
Were we welcomed, where else could our community
Grow, thrive and develop? Where else in or near New Orleans?

That's why many of us reluctantly but nonetheless valiantly
Took on the overthrow of the all-white school board
That educator Mack Spears first integrated, not insignificant
Considering that the Crescent City was the birthplace of
SCLC, the Southern Christian Leadership Conference
And Ming made us young knuckleheads understand the
Significance of controlling our own education and the myriad
Of opportunities associated therewith, long term strategy
Was Ming's forte, anyone could win a dustup or even a mayoral
Election, she taught us to go beyond just winning a battle
When there was a protracted struggle to overcome, which is why
Ming was a leader in championing public healthcare,
Saddle-up warriors she commanded and led the charge
Championing public and affordable healthcare and medications,
A battle that sooner or later we all needed to wage
Whether as patient or advocate, or both

Ming was on it, her dulcet tones gently, and when necessary,
Forcefully waking us up to our responsibilities and opportunities
Ming The Merciless was, is and always will be a major inspiration
For me and countless other New Orleanians woke and aware
Of what time it really is and what we ought to be doing
To confront evil and advance all that it
Good and righteous in this world

All hail Ming The Merciless
All salute Oretha Castle Haley
A woman at the forefront of struggle for
Truth, justice and a truly egalitarian American way

MORNING CALM

For the women of Vietnam, patiently threading together their share, and more, of Third World struggle & solidarity

the eerie bright light
that shatters morning
dawn is the illumination
of bombs

death dropping like
acid rain from unseen
obscene clouds,
a deadly dew
dispensed by invisible
high flying arms

and so began the days
when Nguyen was new,
barely born between napalm runs,
anti-personnel explosives spewing
sinister silverous spikes
with thorny barbs which savagely
struck and cut, searing
into innocent flesh
embedding shrapnel into pliant
pre-pubescent sides, into
soft kidneys and slender
bamboo colored thighs like
gleaming iron fish hooks
piercing a jaw, lancing a gill
or slicing an eye
but who cares now
that the war was lost so
long ago
the high-tech cameras

no longer transmit onto tv sets
into our living rooms
the pain, the unsmelt
stench of flaming bodies or
the barely believable screech
of street side summary executions
as bullets shattered the skulls
of black haired suspected cong
so who cares now
the killers are back home
here in america
where we do not see nor feel
the innumerable silent shells
waiting to explode
upward maiming a peasant's crouch
as ox drawn plow contacts
nor do we cross
oranged wastelands where
nothing green can grow
who cares, now that
the dear johns and joes
are gone, to the victors
have gone the spoilt

who remembers those naked little girls
running down the highway their mouths
silently stretched open in pain
those little girls who are
no longer girls but women now
women whose wombs may never conceive
women who can not dance without pain
women whose scars will not heal
women who can not give birth without surgery
women whose ears can not hear subtle string music
women who can not remember ever having rest

filled sleep during long quiet summer
nights nor sense the tenderness of a lover's
cautious touch caressing what's left of a breast

who cares?

as you struggle in your homeland
a place bombed almost back
"into the stone age"
patiently reconstructing human beings
out of the survivors of war
a prostitute becomes a nurse
an orphan a teacher
a cripple becomes an administrator
and a blind woman an interpreter

Nguyen, it is the work of you
and people like you
which gives soft/strong certainty
to worldwide efforts at
social reconstruction

Nguyen, knowing you helps us
know that we are more
than our past,
less than our future,
neither animals nor gods
but oppressed people who can grasp
tomorrow's dawns and create new days
from bomb cratered yesterdays

in the face of pessimism
your graceful smile
thaws our war hardened hearts

i salute
you who continue, all of you
who inspire hope, whose recovery
encourages all of us victims
to rise and fly like phoenix
ascending out of occidental ashes

i salute
you who move as in a morning sun
rising side by side, always rising,
never stopping, always rising, softly,
always, certainly, softly,
as in a morning
calm

---

author's note:

i do not usually explain my poetry, but this post is special. the context of the poem is important to me. 'morning calm' was written in the late seventies/early eighties and originally conceived as part of a collection of poetry to complement the essays i wrote and published under the title of 'our women keep our skies from falling.'

the plan was to publish a small book with both the poetry and the essays together, but as with so much in life, that never came to pass.

i served in the u.s. army 1965-1968, the vietnam years but i did electronic nuclear missile repair in korea. korea was a major awakening for me about the international aspects of our struggle. i learned a lot from the women in korea, most of whom were prostitutes who lived in a small village just outside the gates of our mountain top base.

i came out of the army fired up and ready to rumble, seeking far more than civil rights. by 1974 i was a delegate to the sixth pan-african conference in dar es salaam, tanzania. the chinese were already working in tanzania. does anyone remember the tan-zam railroad and the effort to break apartheid's economic stranglehold on central and southern africa?

three or so years later, i led a delegation to the people's republic of china. twenty educators and activists from around the united states spent over two weeks traveling throughout china and engaging in serious ideological sessions with chinese comrades. again, my consciousness was raised.

the more i learned about the world and the more people i met who were struggling for self-determination, self-defense, and self-respect, the more i understood that our struggle was truly a global struggle and not simply a racial struggle, or even mainly a pan-african struggle. eventually, i moved away from advocating nationalism as a solution to the issues our people faced. i also became very, very clear that sexism and attendant ills (such as homophobia and heterosexism) was a serious issue that had to be fought both internally and externally.

'morning calm' is then a reflection of my global consciousness and of my anti-sexism advocacy. in 2010, far, far removed from when i wrote this poem i teach vietnamese students in high school. a few of our students were born in vietnam; most of them deal in various ways with the issues of assimilation and retaining their culture, especially their language. this poem was written for the women who are today the grandparents, aunts, and perhaps a few mothers of our students...

one other thing, as i have said numerous times, i use music as my literary model. the rhythms and internal structure of this poem are based on john coltrane's version of 'softly, as in a morning sunrise.'

a luta continua (the struggle continues)...

—kys

my father is dead. again.

(for my father-friend tom dent)

1.

what are fathers
but measuring rods
to gauge our growth

walking canes
to aid our stepping
through vast unknowns

cylindrical vessels
who house ancestral links
the planting of which

into fertile soil
turns today's sorrows
into tomorrow's joys

fathers are more
than mere giants—they are
the "to be" promise

of germinating seed
the genetic baton
passing on

the history of our needs
our deeds, our soul
expressions

2.

i was thousands of miles away
when tom's tree fell

the weight of missing him
answers the age old question

does a falling sound
if no one hears

the crash—yes
i know the answer, yes

because
his aftershock's tremble

reverberates within
the chamber of my skull

at all
the oddest moments

like discovering a special person
within the skin of a child of mine

and discerning at the same time
a lady i used to love

a lady whose love
shaped me

there are periods
when our ability to perceive

presence and potential
is predicated

on having been groomed
by those who have gone before

on having been shown
how to see beyond

what is now
what is known, how

to appreciate the shape
of things to come

all this prescience a product
of learning the living wisdom

of a brusque old man
whose gruffness was so tender

so touching
in its honest intimacy

as he suggested that
there was something beyond

what ever was
and is, and yes, even will be
there is always
something more

something better
to be/come

3.

english words were never meant
to adequately articulate
the anguish in our mouths, our hearts
when we lose the stretching part
of our selves—the stairs we climb
to see further, to descend deeper

as we look out and over
past the limits of horizon line

our vision is improved when we stand
on the shoulders of elders
whose height hoists us higher
than we could ever grow
if we remained flat-footed
married to the ground

the view from these human
balconies enables us to eye
not just near and far
but also back and down
into the wells
of our own personalities

trodding their path
we go beneath the undertow

surveying the superstructure
assaying our foundations
breathing the thin air
of emotional danger
where we are taught to distinguish
the essential differences

between bittersweet and poison
between weariness and resignation
between honesty and cynicism
between maturity and hubris
here, where self-assessment and frankness
are more important than speeches and homilies

if we are fortunate
here we have fathers
who help us
clearly see
depths
as well as distances

4.

in the new orleans
that tom knew
old griots die singing
they do not go silently
into some lonely night

in his new orleans
we do not kill our fathers
to prove that we have arrived

but rather we learn
from them that we can
crack open the kernel
of our own becoming
only by completing
the final maneuver
of life's ultimate passage rite

the step of accepting the torch
and making of ourselves a light
volunteering
to lift the father spirit
to shoulder the responsibility
of becoming beacon
for those newly born
and those yet to come

in our new orleans we do not stop
at simply burying aged bodies
we also dance forward
from funeral line
and accept the awesome
task of filling father shoes

if i really come from
the house of the rising sun,
if i really believe
in resurrection
if i am really
my father's son
i must be reborn
be his life
after death

5.

perhaps a moan
is the most profound
sound one can make
when a father is gone

when my first father died
i cried publicly
this time my tears
for tom are silent
words on paper

the two times
a man is most
alone
are when

he loses
a father and when he
loses his own
life—his
beginning his end

6.

in earth ways
my father is dead. again.

but yet again
he lives

the older i become
the more people i contain

another of my fathers
is dead

long live
my father

long live my father
in me

long live
my many fathers

long live
long live

all the fathers
i am

and all the fathers
i will ever be

On Visiting My Ex-Wife Of 16 Years After Her Third Brain Tumor Operation

1.

they opened your head
to clear the brush growth from your brain

they dug into your skull
to save you

you never doubted your survival
like your name you were ready

stronger than suffering, we shall overcome
evidently your new favorite song

now you re-arrange yourself: hand, heart
head singing together

you construct a new nation
from the older bones

the distant memories and flesh
that refuses to surrender

despair will not dine
on your soul

your will to live is your candle
illuminating whatever dark

chance and circumstance conspired
to descend upon you

your flame rides through those storms
occasionally flickering but ultimately always strong

2.

for a third time you are learning yourself
tasting anew everything you do, motions
you formerly subconsciously made
now require a conscious kick-start
something as simple as walking
can no longer easily be taken for granted

who really remembers tumbling as a baby
people smiling and encouraging you "get up,
get up. you can do it" and embracing you
when you did it—the different sounds
that came out of one's mouth learning to talk
the different items put into one's mouth
learning to taste—who remembers
the struggle to learn how to be who we are?

3.

and so to visit you
in these momentous moments
when regardless of what we see before us
the snapshots inside of us are stronger, more
potent indices, emotional spurs that prod us

i can never forget when you…
do you remember when we…
was yesterday really that long ago

how we have aged
thrown into the sharpest silhouette
as memories pirouette
on today's stage

so

what now? you on one shore
i on another, separated by a river of years
so much water flowing under
so many bridges

what now?

i wave to you from a distant shore
my hand is familiar
my touch is long ago

it hurts to sit in a small room
and be so distant from one who was so close
and so i shake off the cloak of sentimentality
and leave
aware at the back of my mind

that the simple act of saying goodbye
—or more precisely, "tutaonana"

those swahili syllables we taught our children
to recite, not goodbye but we will see each other again

we will see each other again

and the question descends the staircase
with me: when?

that query's younger sibling
innocently posing the more brutal interrogation
"why—do you really want to go through this again?"

4.

by happenstance
i saw gumbi the other day

she asked had i seen you
this was before my visit

i said no
and told her about other issues, other people

close friends literally dying
she shooed away those words

with a curt and cutting response
like they were a fly or an annoying mosquito

ain't none of them
the mother of yall children

5.

and so it goes
trying to make a whole life
out of disparate pieces

parts of a whole puzzle
that do not interlock

my life is a mosaic
full of jagged interruptions

and tayari you are
in both substance and shadow

touching even
when you can only haltingly move
your right hand

our problem

as I back my green pickup out of the driveway, waving
"hola" to my neighbor, on my way
to volunteer at mcdonogh #35 high school, today
is a week after the triumph of trump, and I feel
a similar sadness I felt when we (linda from little rock
and me from new orleans shivering in the cold of minnesota
winter, I pulled the newscast off the teletype, my
hands were shaking, linda was crying as I read aloud
the awful news of malcolm's assassination)—the deed
was horrible, a loss almost unimaginable
except his death was real, we were now in a new era

and time, time is a wheel that only turns forward
no matter what anyone vainly hopes,
we are never going back, never, especially back
to a wished for return to the warmth and security
of the maternal womb, never—no matter
the smiles on our faces in the keepsake photographs
—never a returning of good times recaptured
(is Africa our paradise lost, our
paradise never was?)

we must fight the desire
to be captives of whatever we consider
a grand past, our greatness again, and
again, was not just what we did in some yesteryear
but what, working together, soldiering on
sometimes alone, too often lonely but moving on,
helped along by comrades or a Samaritan
or just a pleasant turn of weather
we must shape/create goodness
out of the madness of these times
within which we live, our task is to overcome

obstacles, vulnerably and valiantly seek love
and unfailingly recognize that if we survive
there is no problem
that we cannot confront, few
problems that we cannot overcome, and
ultimately what we have is the great gift
of a chance, an opportunity to engage
with the world, and maybe,
if we are successful in love and struggle, maybe
we will

OUR WORLD IS LESS FULL NOW THAT MR. FULLER IS GONE

It is always difficult to measure
and certainly impossible to replace
the vital space
that a friend's
final passage leaves

At the funeral site
i viewed the corpse
—and that is what that was,
the man we knew
was not lying there
silent, still and accepting
of circumstance
that was never Hoyt
striding, stirring, agitating—

From somewhere
Hoyt's death reached me
the evening of the notice
of Marley's dying, i remember
i muttered an obscenity,
the certainty of death
for us all does nothing
to lessen the impact
when fighters fall
however, it is our way
that only the forgotten are
truly dead, the remembered
live always inside of us
simply moved to another
plane of existence

I know it is an appropriate
occasion for brilliant phrases
and praise poems
describing his work
and worth, but i don't
feel that right
now, as i watch writers
relatives and friends
view the remains
sadness aches my head
and tastes dry in my mouth

Let us transform this touching grief
before we return to the front
(and hopefully that is where
we all are
headed from here),
let us work as hard as he
stopping only at the
time of our going,
let us retain his memory
chew it like mint
swallow and make muscle of it
and resolve to each of us
secure a portion and recreate Hoyt
whole again rising within
the community
of our carrying on

the past predicts the future

(for narvalee)

when you get closer to yr relatives
you will be surprised

at how black they are,
they feel

the fit and familiarity of their emotions in the twilight
how much of your pain they understand
with a knowing smile, and how much of their pain
you never knew, thus you frown
embarrassed by your ignorance
and turn to yester-world
altared on the mantelpiece:

ancestral photographs, amazingly graceful figures
whose dominant features are boldly ironic eyes
which seemingly float effortlessly just above the surface
of the cream-colored paper, inscriptions in unfading black ink
on the reverse "me & shane, dec. 1934"

a small, soft purple, velvet box enshrining a plain gold ring
a slip of torn paper from another era unthrown-away
seven quickly scribbled numerals, the abacadabra key
to a birth, a midnight move to another town, or even
a pledge cut short by accidental death, "oh, it's just a number,"
the slow, quiet response to your investigation
so you pick up a pencil gilded with the name of a 1947 religious
convention attended and delicately place it down beside
an 87-year-old hand mirror (you resist the impulse
to look at your reflection, afraid that you might see
unfulfilled family aspirations), this mirror is atop
a piece of lace, pressed, folded, ancient matriarchal adornment

you will be surprised to learn,
as the years go on, everything
your people say sounds like something
from your life story, something
you wondered about sitting in the car
the other day in the hospital parking lot before the visit,
before the treatment

especially if you are intelligent
paid more than $10 an hour
carry credit cards rather than cash
and climb aboard a flying machine more than three times a year

you will be surprised that although you live in some other city
there is a spot with your familial name
blind embossed and hand engraved in the heart-home
of people you seldom see, surprised
that much of your life had already been accurately predicted
by an aunt who knew you before you were born, i.e.
when your mother
and father were courting, staying out later than curfew
and clutching dreams tightly in the naked embrace
of yr conception

Remember

even as this world goes mad
let us always remember to remember
we can always choose, always choose life
always choose to love
and to treat other humans
with respect and compassion

to defend ourselves certainly
if and when attacked, but
also, and more importantly,
to extend ourselves to help others

and always, in every way, every
creative way we can conceive, always
to demonstrate with the example
of our every breathing motion
the inspiring power of the positive

positive in our projections
of love
& struggle, love for each
other & creative struggles
to help one another;
struggles to make this world
better and more beautiful

even as the world continues
to go mad
we must creatively continue,
we must remember

Sometimes when i hear thunder, i think of you

your shuddering
intensity

shaking me

like embracing
rumbling
summer thunder

    the lightning
    of your spent smile
    tenderly tattooed
    into the hollow
    of my neck

the feel of you
beneath the pulsing
rain of my rhythms—

    rocking
    like waves

    wetter
    than water

time is a funny thing

there have been times when i found myself with literally nothing
i could do like when i would sit at a stop sign for what seemed
hours trying to figure out how to straighten out the mess i'd
made of my marriage, tayari alone with our five young people &
me alone at a stop sign, & eventually i just crawled on—it's not
like i was the only man who had ever stumbled at that specific
crossroads but when i was there the sun shone all night & i saw
no one's shadow but my own forlorn form tangled in the rocks
& weeds of my emotional life, & although then was years ago,
occasionally i am still shook by an invisible hand, it could be
when i pause in mid-embrace as i hold a comrade from back
in the days i haven't seen in quite a while & they hurl me into
a time machine when they innocently ask with a sincerity so
certain "how are tayari & the kids, they must be grown now?"

there have been times when i felt i was drawing my last breath
& about to bankrupt the bank, especially that sunday morning
we went to face down the klan & the night before those hooded
ones goose-stepping around garish flame cross light had shot at
police in algiers without being arrested which we knew meant
targets were pinned on all our chests but we had to go to high
noon, such poot or get off the pot days give men & women
no choice, & then there was the helpless waiting to exhale of
the pulse pounding pause on the unforgettable creaking bus
stuck to a motionless stop like a lamb patiently awaiting a
slaughter somewhere in the middle of nica. libre between el
rama and managua, the u.s. armed contras on the other side of
the hill, hard working people softly mumbling spanish prayers
& attempting to hide anything that might call attention to
themselves at the bottom a half mile or so from the peak & no
sandinista soldier rescuing cavalry anywhere in sight, & me
frankly more worried about the photos & taped interviews i
might lose than about whether i would die & yet at the same

time after having heard gunfire in the nights i was acutely aware, as fred sanford was fond of seriously joking, that this could be the big one, the one where the bullet singes your skin without so much as an excuse me

there have been times i paused to count the endless ripples on a lake, to note the shape of each leaf on a tree so tall my myopic eyes could not clearly see the top, to merge my being with the azure luminosity of a spring sky, raise my closed eyes to sun warmth & be clearly seen by any passerby as i stand swaying in the breeze mindlessly enjoying the great goodness of nature's beauty

there have been times i have been so harried with details & overwhelmed by minutiae i must have looked like rockefeller's accountant around tax time, dragging myself home mentally exhausted, nia reminds me i started to snore during the month we crammed in a half year's worth of work within six weeks when we did the jazzfest posters in 1993 & have not been able since to shake that sleeping disorder
there have been times i've shared with people events which are now noted in history, our names engraved into the consciousness of both friends & foes so audacious was our doing, we were the flesh levers which moved social mountains, the meaningful moments whose significance sometimes can only be read in hindsight because at the time we were just going with the flow doing what we did & such doing just seemed as right as warm rain & inevitable as darkness following sundown

there have been times when i have made statements so stupid there must have been a poltergeist in my mouth misguiding my tongue, i remember one utterance & each time i remember the cruelty of those words i pause & apologize, a friend was going for her phd at the same time she was dating this man she hoped to make her husband, a hope most of us recognized as a longer shot that a three legged horse beating secretariat in a derby run, but still she was proud of both & in one twisted indiscreet swoop i flung assassin words across a room: "yeah, then"—meaning when she got her phd—"then, you can buy a husband," oh the demons of disorder danced that night i'm sure, my only consolation is that i have not unconsciously done anything as callous as that since, & though i know each of us has been awarded an asshole of the month award for some act whose erasure is fervently desired, knowledge of others fucking up does nothing to dim the blemishes on the resume of my own heart

likewise, there have been times when i've made my ancestors proud, particularly my enslaved african ancestors who courageously & creatively figured ways to squeeze banquets from mustard seeds, times i've proved to be worthy of the sacrifices, guidance, love & understanding showered on me by the union of degreeless first black lab tech at va hospital-new orleans, big val ferdinand, whom friends lovingly called "ferd," with the preacher's daughter, quintessential third grade school teacher, inola, my physical & spiritual earth parents, & most significantly times i've caused a child, i've both fathered & inspired, to stick their chest out or cry joy tears to know that their flesh was connected to mine

but that's the way of the world, one day the weight of my big body will be light as dust, blood gone to rain, spirit gone to ghost, then the meaning of my life will be only in the quality & effects of what i did while traveling through, what creations i birthed, what constructs i destroyed or transformed, i will be measured by what i have meant to others & to the overall health of the earth, those nodes are not just mine but indeed are the arc of each generation & every individual, no matter how each of us consumes our time allotment, chewing cautiously deep in rational thought or wolfing the chow down, savoring the taste of each moment or swallowing several mouthfuls as swiftly as we can, fasting or being gluttonous, focused or totally random, the reality is our matter is only a mere morsel in the mouth of galactic motion, what does the sun care what we do with our little piece so small, so overall futile a wrestling with fate & destiny attempting to shape something significant from the brief ticket we purchase in this crazy lottery of living, only people care & that is the sole true way to identify one's humanness, do we care about being here & care about everyone & everything we encounter in time

time is such a funny thing, whether you think about it or not, whether exciting as tongue kissing an exquisite taboo or boring as olive drab painting of army equipment for the 300th repetition, regardless of what we don't or do, the funny thing is that time is a changing that is constantly the same, is both totally silly & movingly profound, is the depth of blue & the velocity of red, the density of black, the blankness of white & the spectrum scale of all the grays in between, no matter how big a ripple we cause plopping into the cosmic pond eventually the lake's face recomposes into smooth placidity, whether we spill piss or perfume, deposit tears or blood, no matter, the planet receives them all just the same because in the end, just as in the beginning, they all & we all, everything big, little, short & tall, equally slip right on away, ain't it funny?

TOUCH

(for Asinjae Monae Jackson)

we can live together / and still some crazy way
there be a certain wall of silence surrounding personal matters /
    usually
only a few intimacies and renegade thoughts, embarrassing ideas
too risqué or too taboo / to share with others, even blood
close others, or friends who've known us since before we could
    read, not
to mention also with intimate others with whom we share
    physical
nakedness

there is an us that we decline to let others see

except when we honestly write

& even then we try to keep most of our deep interiors / under
the wraps of acceptable thoughts

but

still sometimes

we peek out / something serious escapes

and like a jolt of electricity, say from a toaster when we've stuck a
    butter
knife inside trying to retrieve a small crust of bread / or even the
    static
on a winter day when our woolen slippers on the carpet causes a
    little
spark and we flinch, like that

we touch others and they are surprised / by the force of who we are /
and we in turn are surreptitiously delighted

when they say to us: i never knew
you felt like that

we should consider all of our writing is a kiss, a caress, or even a fist, but
in any case, all cases, if we are true to

our selves our writing is us touching another

We are all amphibians

to/for Chelsey S.
she sees what i saw
& so much more

breathing beneath
water, initially encased
in a placenta
contained
within maternal
flesh until
we outgrew
the pond
and dove to birth
to walk upright
on earth

no matter our solidity
the moon maintains
its pull on us
and we all long
at various
levels of awareness
to float in the tranquility
of a human sea

land is cool
but after all
there is an undertow
we can never escape

it is our nature
we are all amphibians

WE ARE GUILTY OF FORGETTING WHO WE ARE

i am in a room
4 walls, ceiling, floor
2 windows, a door
outside the window is the world
no walls, sky, earth
death, birth, & the relative briefness of life
inside is the same as outside
only smaller, less complex
outside is the same as inside
only bigger, more choices & possibilities

there are only three questions to ask/to answer
1. who am i, 2. what is the world
& 3. how do i change, love or leave it

nothing else except
maybe
    god sitting somewhere
    marveling at our transformation, god
    mystified, unable to explain the logic
    of how we have become just like
    the pseudo-human creatures
    who enslaved our ancestors

    wow

    after all the centuries of racist bullshit,
    lynchings, chattel slavery & such that
    we black people have suffered
    who would have thought

that violent savages
& impotent religious fanatics
is what we would be come

wow

"WE MUSTN'T CRY, WE MUST CONTINUE!"

(a poem for latin/spanish/sister comrade
Beatriz Allende, whose death
12 Oct. 77 has been classified
as a suicide)

I. WE MUSTN'T CRY

8 Oct. 1967
bulletin
bullets in him
the doctor is dead
bulletin
Che Guevara is dead
is dead
bulletin
they said
"raise his head,
cut his hands,
let the whole world watch"

11 Sept. 1973
the poor are pushed back into their "places"
the proletarian palace is pulverized
the bespectacled physician/president
    with the incongruous hard hat on
    is finally finished off, at last
chile is cold again, again a safe
haven for pullers of fingernails
and militant mutilators of genitals,
of generations
pentagon generals politely applaud
wall street winks, sighs
deep in ITT
a brief missive settles

"START. Business as Usual.
START."

5 Oct. 1974
the news probably came
glaring over a short wave
dressed in nothing
but the brutal bottom line

the much sought
finally caught
terrorist "revolutionary"
Miguel Enríquez,
Secretary General of the
Movement of the Revolutionary Left
(MIR) the outlawed and
banned communist group
has been shot
dead in Chile

II. WE MUST CONTINUE

11 Oct. 1977
Habana
looking back in stony silence
Beatriz does not turn

a woman
surveys the casualties
entombed in her mind:

is this maddening life-extinguishing
exile what I was reserved to
be a showpiece of a rusted revolution
a woman who vainly waits, keeping female

faith in a stone that's gone to dust like
our male seed scattered
revolutionary cemeteries have created
an incredible metamorphosis
I too have become a man
or what you mean when you
say "man," have already
done all that our men do
except die—I am dying,
but I have not died yet
but, yes, like all the others
I'll gladly drink my bitter cup
spare me nothing

a woman?
yes/no, a mother, a
physician, a lover, a
revolutionary, a
flesh, a mind, a
feeling, a deed, I
don't mind dying
if that's what it takes
to continue, Che continued
Allende my sire,
Miguel my guide, and
now, and now I

outside somewhere someone is waiting
for me to speak, it's rally time again
bring out the bereaved widow
of socialism, not I any longer,
not I, now
it's my turn to continue
I must continue on
and meet this end

We Say, Bechet

they say Bechet
was the only man born
whose solos could silence Louie Armstrong
by simply the awesome strength of melodious song
    ringing resplendent in dulcet tones
    through the bell of Sidney's serpentine saxophone

    they say Bechet
    was a Creole colored Black man
    who ventured forth to France land
    to get closer to Africa his beloved
    albeit estranged ancestral homeland

    they say Bechet
    was an hombre of straight backed pride
    with a quick silver temper he seldom bottled inside
    and the swiftness of a pugilist in his ability to settle scores
    and, mano a mano, to batter open doors

they say Bechet
    was possessed by the gris gris of his grandfather
    who had impassionately danced beneath tall oak trees
    in the sunshine of Sunday breeze
    during weekly place de Congo gatherings
    and that this same Bechet directly inspired the afro-blue
        blowing
    of Coltrane's adoption of the gypsy drone
    that undulating high pitched moan
    articulated in spirit conjuring tongues & shot flickering hot
    out of the damballa tubing of a b-flat soprano saxophone

they say Bechet
when they don't know what else to say
Bechet when they speak admiringly
of an exotic untamed noir beauty
Bechet when they search diligently
for lions within the aural jungles of the 20th century
Bechet of the sweeping vibrato undammable
as the torrential flow of the mighty Mississippi
Bechet of amazingly graceful creativity
fierce as the hand wrought iron filigrees
of Black diasporan new world melodies

Bechet, Bechet, Bechet
is what they say
when they mean to mark the beginning,
the genesis of the Black man's astonishing
affair d'amour with the hybrid horn
Adolphe named the saxophone

Bechet they say
oh how seriously huge this gigantic petite fleur played
this majestic musicianeer Bechet
whose mournfilled joy remains today
the birth cry of Black music's jazz ascendency
Bechet, Bechet, Bechet
we say

what can i say?

(to friends who have separated)

breaking apart two who had become one seems criminally
wrong nevertheless there are those of us who
can not stay once love has gone

it deeply hurt me to deeply hurt my ex
but i did, and, because i did, i know
the cruel charity of not staying when i realized "i had to go"

there is a loneliness that doesn't desire company
a weariness which sleep can never erase
here we unavoidably lick the lead of our failures, a taste
which poisons the sweetness of every yesterday

i continue to love you both dearly and will miss
your wholeness surely—what more need be said?

when one heart is broken both sides are bloodied—it is
impossible to talk to one without thinking of the other

WHAT DOES YOUR LIFE MEAN TO A TREE?

for Ken Devine paraphrasing Jefferson Airplane

1.
why would anybody want to be a picture/a snapshot
of random confusion masquerading
as a 20th century American citizen
a guest on montel explaining why, contrary to most
males, you masturbate with your left hand

we americans watch television more than
we watch trees or observe the leaves
shaking in the breeze, it would be hip
to live life like in a movie is what
some of us actually believe/but dig
life is not something you watch
from a sitting position with chips & a beer lite
life, like music, is a great goodness
you birth, be godlike & create

2.
some one once asked me "what do you do for a living?"
"for a living?" i said, "hmmmmm, well i

dream, write
make love
create, dream, make love
every chance i get
work, dream
make love, help others do the same
that's what i do: work, dream
make love
to live is to dream, to work
to make. . ."
you get the picture?

after all life is too hard not to live
once given the opportunity
plus when you step into tomorrow & dance
before ra's arkestra within the purview
of eternity, & your steps are cross-examined, an inquisitor
is going to hold up what you did & ask you did you do that
& ask you what good is your life to a tree/cause you know
trees are some hip, hip creatures & their wellbeing
is the ultimate measure of our passing thru

> & you better be prepared to answer something besides
> some shit like "well, i'll be some good ass
> fertilizer now that i'm dead. . ."

Why I am not Hindu
(karma revisited)

I cannot be this dumb
Not to have learned from doing
This before

Not just the mistakes
But also the certainties
Which are what?

Knowing anything?
What can we know? We think
We know

But can we
Catch wind in a box
Live life better than before?

The trouble is no one
Knows, none of us survive
We all live, how-so-ever

We all die, how-so-ever
What difference does our living make
To the sun, the stars

The sky above, the earth?
Whatever we think we know
Is solely what we think

The only certainty
Is death, everything else is
Subject to change

YESTERDAY WAS SO BEAUTIFUL #2 (and its passing so sad)

/in memory, in heart for Gloria Firmin and so many others encountered along the way

1.
when the day transitions
it goes to night
first, before
there can be another
day

sometimes
a day has been
so beautiful
that in the night
instead of looking
forward
to another day
we can only grieve
for what is gone

but each day
is its own being
each being
has their own
day

whatever beauty
we find missing
tomorrow, whatever
we might miss
from yesterday

well, that beauty
we must become

tomorrow
we must be
as beautiful
as the departed day
we mourn in the anguish
of night

2.
ultimately, our beauty
the heart we extend to others
the way we transform the mundane
successfully make butterfly wings
out of this world's ordinary caterpillar
toils and troubles, shake off inevitable
disasters and overcome the multitude of ongoing
bills and debt as we undertake long marches
survive treacherous journeys to meet, duel and
deal with the man, hard dances we do with the devil
the cost of admission to the grand balls of our times
and oh we so do love to dance, absolutely adore
making music, breaking sweet bread
with bosom buddies and laughing
while embracing close family, friends
and the multitude of others, the fellow pilgrims
we encounter while passing through
economic slaughter, wading across dirty political
waters, raging red, whites and blues,
these seas that too often flood our lives

this is our duty: use the hammer of beautiful
yesterdays to sculpt and shape the troubled rocks
of today into tomorrow's beauties, procreate

inspirations for generations yet to come, give birth
to the most sacred homages we can conceive
honoring ancestral legacies and the memories
of those whose hands we had the joy of holding
as we made our moves, sang our songs, fought
our fears, and freely dedicated our lives
to encouraging ourselves and others to do
all that we can, all that we
are capable of doing to make
this world a better and more beautiful
place than when we first arrived upon
this bitter earth which we make sweet
using the force of our kisses and work, our
deepest love and daily struggle

You can't survive on salt water
-seven haiku for old orleans-

1.
dead dogs hang from trees
bloated barges sit on the
wrong side of levees

2.
dumb pigeons have flown
now it's people's turn to perch
roasting atop roofs

3.
a caravan of
yellow busses drowns because
the mayor can't drive

4.
official death counts
exclude so-called looters shot
on sight of their skin

5.
dry folk uptown hold
their noses, rejecting wet
people's funky stank

6.
things that go bump in
the night: your boat against a
dead baby's body

7.
a son returns, finds
four-month old bones wearing his
missing mother's dress

You'll Never See My Byline In The Times-Picayune

Asante, the eldest of five siblings, sent me an email early, early
this morning citing a photo of me and five comrades
striding out of city hall, fists upraised—we had taken over
the mayor's office: Ernest Morial, the first black mayor.

Around our necks we wore signs, each with the name
of a person murdered by the police in the west bank
    neighborhood
known as Algiers (at least the colonialists are consistent,
They always kill some of us to try to discourage the rest of us).

I know we are in a post-racial state, I know today is not
as murderous as yesterday except if you understand
that black homicide is really genocide and is as high as a hawk
patrolling the sky. Anyway, the article gave no context—

we were just crazy, young niggers—overlook the white boy
with us (besides he was probably one of those Jewish radicals),
and that girl must have been the consort of one of us
otherwise why would a woman protest? I smiled
and called my daughter to thank her for passing the info on.
Asante said she remembered those days, she was maybe ten or
    eleven
but she remembered and she asked herself the right questions:
"what now?" "what am I doing for the greater good?"

"when? will the imbalance between haves and have nots
ever be able to really change?" I smiled. Asante was part
of the reason we resorted to direct action. I wanted to give
her (and all other young people) something stronger, something

more than my name in the daily paper endorsing bullshit
cooperating with capitalism, suit&tied down, a negro
the white folks could be proud of. I wanted to be the question
mark in the eyes of the status quo: what in the world

do those negroes want? Don't they have a black mayor?
Isn't that enough/too much? How come they smiling,
looking so happy? Shouldn't they have been arrested?
What is the world coming to? Can't we bring back

the good old days when there was respect
for law and order? I know we should never forget
the law and order that brought us here, that
stole this land, killed off the native inhabitants

and fucked with our minds so much
that some of us would love to do nothing so much
as write our own obituaries—yes, I know
I sound extreme but that's how I responded to murder.

COMPLETE INDEX OF POEMS

**appears or is referenced in an essay*